For Colum,

I hope you enjoy this as much as I enjoyed writing it. Thank you for your friendship.

Peace & Love,
John A. Brennan
9/20/14

Don't Die with Regrets

Regrets

Ireland and the Lessons My Father Taught Me

John A. Brennan

Dedication

For Mal

It is my belief that we are the product of a vast gene pool that has been passed down to us through the ages, by our ancestors. This wealth of information is within each one of us, and can be tapped into at any time. Who they were makes us, largely what we are. While it is an accepted fact that our upbringing and social status have a great impact on us in our formative years, that is to say, until we reach the age of reason at seven years old, it has only a partial effect on who we really are and more importantly, who we are becoming. For a man to know himself, understand why he thinks, acts and reacts as he does, he must first know where he came from, have a good knowledge of his cultural heritage, the history of the land in which he was born, and who his ancestors were. He must also know and understand his own father.

As a child, growing up, it appeared that my father's main intention was to raise my awareness so that I would try to always follow the right path and be ready for whatever life had in store for me. I must confess that in my humble and sometimes futile attempts to follow his sage advice, I managed to raise more than a few eyebrows. I have lost count of the number of glasses I have raised over the years, as well as the many hackles. In my youthful years, I must admit that I have raised quite a few skirts also. Thankfully, for the most part, his plan worked. His single, most profound piece of advice was passed on to me as he lay on his deathbed. He had been ill for a year and each evening after work I would stop by and visit with him. One evening I climbed the stairs and entered his bedroom, he was laying down and appeared to be asleep.

As I sat in the chair at his bedside, he opened his eyes and a smile crossed his dried lips. "Ahhh, is that you son?" "Yes dad, it's me. How are you feeling tonight?" "Very weak, I think I'll be leaving here soon." He struggled bravely to sit upright and after a huge effort leaned over, grabbed my arm tightly and whispered hoarsely, "Son, whatever you do, ***don't die with regrets***." He lay down then and closed his eyes. Those were the last words he ever uttered. Two days later, he passed away.

I hope this book will make the reader think, laugh, and perhaps shed a tear or two. More importantly, I hope it will inspire you to follow your dreams no matter how many obstacles you encounter along life's journey. It is better to try, even if only to fail sometimes, than not try and then live a lesser life and die with regrets. I dedicate this collection of short stories and poems to my Father and I invite you to embark on this journey with me as your guide. A journey, which started long before the day I entered this earthly realm, and is still ongoing.

The author's father, Mal at age 21.

Author, John A. Brennan at age 19.

Foreword

This I wrote as a tribute to all writers, musicians and artists, who from time to time experience bouts of what I call the nasty, malodorous S.S.E. (shitty self-esteem). Consider this as a pat on the back, as I, hope to encourage us all that it is indeed more rewarding to pursue a creative path. In my experience, such a journey will no doubt lead to a life of greater satisfaction and fewer regrets.

All artists, writers, musicians, and poets have the uncanny ability to tap into the realm of spirit. We have been given a gift that enables us to transcend the mundane, experience the world as we see and feel it, and know how it should be. We have the ability to turn what to most people, are chaotic thoughts and feelings, into beautiful and meaningful works of art. Despite having to live and survive in the material world, we are blessed with the grace that enables us to never stray far from our original nature.

We pass on what we have learned through our words, which are the manifestation of our collective knowledge. It is a shamanistic quality, which we possess. If we believe as I do that, we are gifted and we believe that a gift only works when we give it away willingly, then it is our duty to pass it on. All cultures revere their artists, none more so than my own, the Irish. We call them Seanacchie (shan-a-key) the storytellers, the bards and the minstrels.

John

Acknowledgments

I could never have attempted to write this book without the help of many individuals both living and long departed. My earliest influences were the men in the middle of the fifth. Century AD, the monks and scribes, who, against all odds had the foresight and tenacity to painstakingly collect, translate and record for the future generations the ancient manuscripts not destroyed in that brutal period of history known as the *dark ages*.

I owe a huge debt of gratitude to the Irish writers and poets O'Casey, Joyce, Shaw, Wilde, Yeats, Pearse, and Behan etc. for their lifelong inspiration, which has transcended the ages. I am also deeply indebted to the musicians who always lifted my spirit and made me proud to be an Irishman. Van Morrison, Christy Moore, U2, Sinead O'Connor, Rory Gallagher, Thin Lizzy and the Boomtown Rats are but a few of those individuals who keep the spirit of the Seannachie (storyteller) alive by sending their words and music out into the ether to delight and educate the world.

One of my earliest teachers, Kevin McMahon, was the first to encourage me to write as a young boy in primary school in Crossmaglen and I wish to thank him sincerely.

Women have and still do, play a vitally important role in my life, without their feminine love, guidance, and patience it is doubtful that I could ever have survived. They always seemed to appear at the various stages in my life, just when I needed them most. I cite my mother Ellen a loving, patient, kind, and supportive woman who instilled a sense of humility in me at an early age. My wonderful sisters, Teresa, Marion, and Frances who believed in me when I doubted myself. Nancy, the beautiful girl I left behind. Kay, my long-suffering wife of twenty-five years, who loved, supported and guided me through the madness. Joanne, my beautiful daughter, who replaced Mark Anthony, the son I lost. Kathy and Galina, those two beautiful women who entered my life specifically to love and enable me to travel and fulfil my dreams. To Dalin, the little Indian girl, whose innocent, childlike manner sustained and comforted me through the roughest period in my life. To them all I offer my sincere gratitude and heartfelt love.

To my uncle Joe who was like a second father to me and always took my side, and told me not to worry, that "youth must always have its fling." To my relatives the Flynn's, Johnny, Vincent, and Jimmy, those tall, brave men who taught me how to stand up for what I believe in, at any cost, and be a true man. To Pat Hearty who showed me that like him, I am indeed multi-talented. To Michael Brennan Sr. without whose invitation to come and visit him in New York, my life would have taken a very different route. To them all I offer a humble thank you.

A sincere thank you to Debbi Honoroff at Hofstra University and their stellar writing programs for enabling me to explore and develop my dormant skills. Two writing groups of which I am a proud member have always encouraged and motivated me: The Long Island Writers Guild, whose president Dennis T. Kotch and his wife Beverley always supported my efforts. The Amateur Writers of Long Island's Steve Sanderson and Varteny Koulian deserve a pat on the back for their skillful guidance and positive critique of my works. I am forever indebted to the Performance Poets Association of Long Island organizer Cliff Bleidner and event hosts Lorraine Conlin and Vicki Iorio for providing me with a forum in which to express, through the spoken word, my stories, and poetry, to live audiences.

To The Walt Whitman Birthplace in Huntington, Long Island of which I am a humble member, a hearty thanks for inviting me in. To Mr. George Wallace, ringmaster, event organizer extraordinaire and shining beacon throughout the worldwide poetry community, I owe many pints of Guinness. To James Paul Wagner and staff at Local Gems Press, a sincere thank-you for your commitment to the Bardic tradition. To the Bardess in residence Ms. Judy Turek a hug of gratitude for her kind encouragement. A special word of gratitude for Giovanni Corvinus and Chris Nicola, hosts of the monthly poetry readings held at The Roast Coffee and Tea Company, Patchogue, Long Island for their wonderful friendship and support.

To Russ Green and his stellar Greens Revolution, a hearty slap on the back for keeping the spirit of the Beats alive and screaming. To Mary Jane Tenerelli, hostess at Caffe Portofino, Northport, Long Island for her valiant efforts in keeping the spoken word alive. To Margarette Wahl, hostess at Bellmore Bean Café, Bellmore, Long Island a big hug and thank you. To

Kelly J. Powell hostess at BJ Spoke Art Gallery, Huntington, Long Island for her friendship and warm smile. To Ed Luhrs for reminding me that indeed, language does transcend the ages and that the ukulele is indeed a special instrument, a big nod of gratitude to all.

To Erica and John Paul and their amazing staff at Cornucopias' Noshery in Amityville, Long Island, thank you for always making me welcome and feeding me. To Tom Paul and everyone at Sip This, Valley Stream, Long Island for their hospitality toward artists of all kinds. Thank you to event host, Doreen D. Spungin for putting up with my ranting and ravings, and allowing me to be me. To Mr. John Walsh and the Irish Cultural Society, Garden City, Long Island a round of applause for keeping the Irish spirit alive and kicking in New York. And to all of the many other event coordinators who have welcomed me in to their wide family of poets, writers and performers I say humbly, thank you, thank you all.

To my agent Diane Martin, CEO at Escribe Publishing Company, who encouraged, guided, and boosted my self-esteem greatly when she agreed blindly, to publish my book, I offer my heartfelt thanks.

And lastly, to the Grande Dame herself, Ms. Barbara Reiher-Meyers, the *doyen* of the Long Island Poetry community, a big kiss and a hug. Barbara was instrumental in dragging me, kicking and screaming over to the *dark side*, known fondly as *Poetry,* and without her encouragement, it is doubtful that I would ever have gotten this far. Her magnificent words of encouragement, *'Shut up and just read the bloody poem'* still ring in my ears and help me keep my feet firmly planted on *Terra Firma.*

Escribe Publishing Inc.

"We're challenging all the rules about who gets to be published, because to write is to live one's dreams."

Diane L. Martin
President and Chief Executive Officer

Come Write for Us

On the Web

http://www.escribepublishing.com

TABLE OF CONTENTS

Illustrations

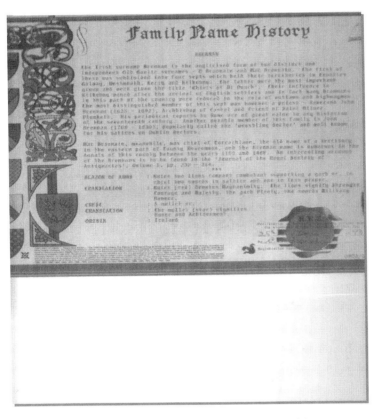

Brennan Family Name History and Coat of Arms
Royal Society of Antiquaries of Ireland

Ireland's Lough Ross at Sunset

Don't Die with Regrets

Ireland and the Lessons My Father Taught Me

"Over in Kilkenny"

"Many years ago"

"Me Father sang a song to me."

John A. Brennan

CHAPTER 1

A Brief History of Ireland and The Brennans

According to the writings in many of the ancient Annals, much of the world, including Ireland, was covered with vast ice sheets until approximately 10,000 years ago. As the ice slowly retreated, it carved the island into the shape that it is today. Once the weight and pressure of the ice was no longer a factor the earth sprang back and major volcanic activity took place. When these eruptions finally ceased the earth cooled, water rose to the surface and became the lakes and rivers that today we all know and love. What I am attempting to relate are my own early recollections of my father and the deep impact he made on me as both a child and later, as a man. To do this, I realized that I had to start at the beginning. This meant that somehow I had to travel back in time to the distant age before my father's people, the Celts, first entered Ireland. To accomplish this daunting task, I have relied heavily on the writings of Michael O'Cleary, a Franciscan monk, who, with three other scholars, compiled what has collectively become known as the *Annals of The Four Masters*.[1] They were written in the Franciscan Friary in Donegal town between 1632 AD and 1636 AD. These annals are a compilation of the ancient writings that were saved from destruction. They tell the story of Ireland from the end of the last ice age to the mid 1600's. From the 1600's forward, I have relied on the writings of Geoffrey Keating in *The Book of Invasions*.

Admittedly, this is **_not_** the work of an academic; it is a humble attempt by a man who feels deeply connected to and influenced by his ancestors.

---

[1] "Annals of the Four Masters." *Wikipedia: The Free Encyclopedia*. Wikimedia Foundation Inc., 6 Oct. 2007. Web.5 Mar. 2012.

The first humans arrived in Ireland around 9000 years ago. They are believed to have crossed land bridges that still existed at that time. One connected southeastern Ireland and southwestern Britain. The other connected County Antrim in northeastern Ireland with the west coast of Scotland. The land bridges later disappeared as the sea level rose. Across these land bridges came various hunter-gatherers whose numbers were so small that they made little impact and soon died out from disease and starvation. Several species of wild animals migrated around this time also. The most notable of these animals was the giant elk. The elk was almost big as an elephant and a perfect specimen can be seen in the National Museum in Dublin.

Recently, fossil remains of extremely large bears have been found in caves in Ireland that suggest by means of DNA sampling, that they are the forebears of our modern Polar bear. There is archaeological evidence that County Antrim was the favored area of habitation at this time. This northern part of Ireland was the only source of flint, which the stone-age people utilized as tools, arrowheads, and spear points. These hunter gatherers lived mostly along the coasts, ate fish and fowl and rarely ventured inland. Ireland was covered in dense oak and ash forests at this time. As the sea level rose, the larger animals became trapped; they subsequently became extinct. This period became known as the Mesolithic stone age.

The first individually _named_ humans to make an impact in Ireland were Cessair, a daughter of the biblical Noah's son Bith and his wife Birren, who were denied a place on the Ark. They literally missed the boat! Cessair, together with three men and fifty women, set sail on their own. After seven years, they arrived in Bantry, County Cork sometime before the great flood. It is believed that Cessair is buried at the summit of Knockmaa, near Tuam,

County Galway. Their numbers were too small to inhabit all of the land.

The Fomorians were the next to arrive. They were reportedly seafarers, possibly pirates. It is believed that they originally came from Northern Africa, as they have been described as having dark hair and skin. By all accounts, they were a warlike and troublesome people. Two brothers ruled their followers with iron fists.

A group led by Partholon, a son of Sera the King of Greece, came next. This is the first mention of royalty in Irish history. This group was the first to arrive after the time of the *great flood*. It was during this time Newgrange passage tomb was built along with many other stone mounds, cairns, and passage graves. *The Book of Invasions* gives us a little more information stating that Partholon and one thousand followers came to Ireland via Greece, Sicily, and Anatolia arriving roughly about 300 years after the *great flood*.[2] At the time of their arrival, there were three lakes, nine rivers, and one large plain. Their numbers grew to approximately four thousand but were eventually to become victims of a plague. It is believed that Parthalon fought the Fomorians in the first battle on Irish soil. Parthalon cleared four more plains and seven more lakes formed.

When the Nemedians arrived, Ireland had been largely uninhabited for thirty years following the deaths of Parthalon's last followers. Some small pockets of Fomorians still survived but they were defeated by Nemed in three epic battles. The surviving Fomorians were driven back and moved out onto Tory Island off the west coast. Nemed arrived in Ireland having left the Caspian Sea area, with a fleet of forty-four ships. After they had travelled for a year and a half, they arrived in Ireland with only one ship. He

---

[2] "The Book of Invasions." *Wikipedia: The Free Encyclopedia*. Wikimedia Foundation Inc., 10 Dec. 2008. Web.7 Mar. 2012.

founded two Royal Forts and cleared twelve large plains. He and three thousand of his people later died from the effects of a plague. Nemed was buried on the hill of Ard Nemid on Great Island in Cork Harbor.

The Fir Bolg makes their appearance in Ireland. It is believed that they originated in Greece, where they captured the ships belonging to their masters and put to sea. They eventually reached Gaul, Britain and Belgium. It is thought that they were conquered by the Gaels and made serfs by them. They wore the garb of subjects, namely, breeches. Loosely translated *Fir Bolg* means *breeches wearers*. Anyone not considered serfs wore tunics and cloaks. The Fir Bolg were ejected from Ireland at one point, but returned some time later from Scotland, with a leader called Aengus. This episode is loosely referred to as a Pictish invasion. They were given the Aran Islands on which they settled. There are remnants of a fortress on Inishmore related to Aengus and the Fir Bolg. With the Fir Bolg came the first quasi-Celtic influence.

Now our history becomes more interesting. The Tuatha De Danann arrives. The name translates to *peoples of the Goddess Danu*. They were the descendants of Nemed. They brought with them the art of the supernatural and among their possessions, it is said they brought four magical treasures: the Dagda's cauldron, the spear of Lugh, the stone of Fal, the Sword of light of Nuada. Epic battles were fought against the remnants of the Fir Bolg and the remaining Fomorians. They were led by their King Nuada and they fought the Fir Bolg in two great battles and defeated them. Many of the myths and legends that we are all familiar with started to take root at this time. Lugh, the Tuatha champion was then crowned king.

Next, came the Milesians led by Ith who was the son of a Scythian father named Goidel Glas and who, it is said, was present at the fall of the

Tower of Babel, and whose mother Scota, was a Pharoah's daughter. She was rumored to be a daughter of Rameses the Great, who sired over one hundred offspring. They left Egypt around the time of the exodus of Moses and eventually settled in the Iberian Peninsula (Galicia and Northern Portugal). Legend has it that Ith first saw Ireland from the top of Hercules tower in Galicia. (He must have had excellent eyesight). Epic battles were fought between the Milesians and the Tuatha De Dannan. Eventually, a deal was struck whereby the land was divided, with the clever Milesians getting the *above ground* and the Tuatha the *underground*. It is from this time we start to hear the stories about the *little people* and the *fairies*.

The practice of farming had spread from the Middle East through eastern and southern Europe and reached the British Isles around 6000 years ago. It arrived in Ireland with the settlers who came next, 5500 years ago. These Neolithic people brought goats, sheep, and cattle. They also brought wheat and barley. One very important discovery was Porcellanite. It is a stone harder and more durable than flint, which the Mesolithic people had used. With axes made from a harder stone, the upland forests could be cleared effectively. Thus, in the Neolithic stone age, basic farming began in Ireland.

The discovery of metal was a major turning point in human history. This new technology arrived in Ireland 4000 years ago. It is believed that settlers from France (Gaels?) brought it with them and slowly the existing inhabitants learned how to mix copper and tin. These two cultures merged and gave birth to the Irish Bronze age.

John A. Brennan

The Celts

The Celts began arriving in Ireland around 2500 years ago. It was during this period that my ancestors, the O'Brannains arrived in Ireland. One of the major advantages the Celts possessed was their discovery of Iron. They came in such large numbers that within a few hundred years of their arrival, they either obliterated or assimilated the existing cultures. It is thought that as the Romans moved slowly westward, the Celts moved ahead of the legions and some of these tribes ended up in Ireland. They could not retreat further. Hibernia, as Ireland became known as, was their last bastion. With these Celts came a tribe called the Romanies. They it is said had the gift of second sight. A priestly sect known as Druids also migrated with the main body of Celts and would eventually have a huge impact on the direction that Irish culture took from this time. Ireland and the area of Scotland north of Hadrian's Wall were never conquered by the Romans. The Romans did setup up trading posts in Ireland but not until approximately 100 AD. It appears that the Romans influenced the language of at least one Celtic clan in Munster as they spoke Latin. The ancient Ogham was the first written script in Ireland and was based on the Latin alphabet. It resembled a runic style of writing, but distinctly Celtic. [3]

After the fall of the Roman Empire, the greater part of Europe descended into utter chaos and this period became known as the *dark ages*. Anarchy ruled, all learning waned, and book burning was common. Ireland however, being an insular island, ignored all of this and continued to flourish academically and intellectually. Scholar monks, fluent in Latin, Greek, and Hebrew with their foresight and unremitting dedication, kept

[3] Abbot, Patrick. "Prehistoric and Celtic Ireland." Web. *Wesley Johnston*. Wesley Johnston, 28 12 2002. Web. 6 Mar 2012.

scholarship alive. Ireland in the fifth century was the center of scholastic learning. The term *Land of Saints and Scholars* describes this perfectly, for that is what Ireland was then and still is today.

Christianity

Christianity, it is widely believed, had already taken a tentative foothold in Ireland before Patrick arrived. Ciaran (the elder) had preached it in the late 4th Century AD and was the first bishop of Ossory. In 430 AD, Pope Celestine had sent a Bishop named Palladius to Ireland. His mission was to minister to any that were already Christianized by that time. Paganism was practiced by all of the Celtic tribes and ministered by a priest-like sect called Druids. It was the main belief system at that time. These were the *holy men* of the Celtic peoples and, indeed, commanded great respect among them but were seen as the obstacle to the new religion. [4]

Patrick, a newly appointed Bishop, on his return to Ireland in 432 AD, recognized this and knew that he would have to convert the Druids first. He felt that this would be the best way to reach the masses. That was the genius of Patrick. He favored assimilation rather than coercion. It is reported that several attempts were made on his life. Patrick was born in Roman Britain in 387 AD. His father Calpornius, was a deacon, his grandfather Potitus, a priest. In 403 AD, as a young Roman boy of sixteen, he was taken captive by Celtic raiders from his home on the West coast of Britain and brought to County Antrim, where he became a shepherd for the local Chieftain.

By his own account, for six years he lived a lonely life on the slopes of

---

[4] Ibid.

the extinct, volcanic, Slemish Mountain. Patrick wrote about his experiences later, in two letters that have survived. Raiding was a regular occurrence and, during these raids, livestock and slaves would be taken. In his sixth year of captivity he writes, "I heard a voice that told me a ship was waiting to bring me home." He left his master and journeyed many miles to a port where a ship awaited, and sometime later, he reached his home and family.

The Vikings

Toward the end of the eighth. Century AD, Ireland was completely Gaelic. It was a mostly rural society with no towns or cities and the only large settlements were small hamlets that grew up around Monasteries. The Monastery was firstly, the seat of learning but was also involved in the cultural, economic, and political affairs of its province. In the seventh. Century AD the O'Neill clan were the ruling dynasty, divided into two separate clans, the Northern and Southern O'Neil, each controlling half of the country. The first raid by the Vikings was recorded in 795 AD when Lambay Island was looted. It is widely believed that they came out of the Fjords of Norway in Long-ships. That first raid was the beginning of two hundred years of intermittent warfare, and pillage. Towards the end of the ninth. Century AD, the island was almost completely Christian with monasteries the favored targets, but these raiders spared no one. The Vikings were eventually defeated by King Brian Boru at the battle of Clontarf in 1014. [5]

---

[5] Ibid.

The Norman Invasion

Malachy Brennan, my father, was a descendant of one of two clans who arrived in Ireland approximately two thousand five hundred years ago, after separating from the larger wave of an amalgam of migrating Celts. Once in Ireland, they divided into four septs. Mal, as he became fondly known, was of the Mac Brannain clan but they later replaced the *Mac* with *O* as a means of distinguishing their sept and therefore became O'Brannain. This sept settled mainly in County Kilkenny where they were granted lands and given the title, *Chiefs of Ui Duach*. This area was known as the kingdom of Ossory. They were, to quote Geoffrey Keating in the *Book of Invasions*, a noble clan by all accounts, forthright, honest, and chivalrous. They were distinguished by their military achievements and were some of the most renowned champions of the times in which they lived. Many scholars have often speculated as to when the British first invaded Ireland. This is how it happened.

The dispossession of Diarmait Mac Murchada, the High king of Leinster, from his lands by the High king of Munster, Ruari O'Connor, eventually led to the ouster of the O'Brannains from their lands and the start of serious hardship and wars that continue to the present day. To recover his kingdom, Mac Murchada enlisted the aid of Henry II of England. That, as the fella says, is when the nightmare began. Mac Murchada left Ireland in 1166 and travelled via Bristol, England to Aquitaine, France, where he met with Henry II. Henry could not help him at that time but gave him an open letter of introduction. He was eventually and some would say fatefully, granted a meeting with Richard de Clare, one of Henry's top aides. This noble character was the son of Gilbert de Clare, the first Earl of Pembroke.[6] Richard, affectionately known as *Strongbow*, was out of favor with Henry II at that time for taking King Stephen's side in a battle against Henry's mother, the Empress Matilda. I am not sure if this Matilda was ever known to have waltzed, but I digress. Because of his treachery, Richard could not inherit his father's title, but endowed himself with the name *Strongbow*.

Richard de Clare and Diarmait Mac Murchada met in 1168. A deal was struck between two upright citizens whereby for De Clare's assistance with an army, he would be given the lily-white hand (and presumably a whole lot more) of Aoife, Mac Murchada's blushing, eldest daughter. More importantly, Richard would be in line for the Kingship of Leinster through marriage. An army was assembled which included companies of Welsh and Flemish archers. This invasion army was led by Raymond Fitzgerald and in quick succession; it overwhelmed the Viking established towns of Wexford, Waterford, and Dublin in 1169-1170. Strongbow did not take part in these battles and only arrived in Ireland when the dust had settled, in late 1170. In 1171, Mac Murchada died and his son Donal claimed the Kingship under the ancient Brehon Laws. *Strongbow* was having none of that and as he had already ravished the fair Aoife, (they did not call him *Strongbow* for nothing), he claimed the Kingship as his right by marriage. Soon after, Ruari O'Connor led an army against *Strongbow*. He was however, driven back. O'Connor and the remains of his army retreated to Galway. Meanwhile, Henry, back in England began to get worried about the success *Strongbow* was having and decided to invade Ireland himself. This he did in 1172 and claimed the title, Lord of Ireland. Richard was stripped of his title at that time. Henry II signed the Treaty of Windsor in 1175 and under the terms,

---

[6] Ibid.

Ruari O'Connor was granted the Kingdom of Ireland, minus Leinster, Meath, Dublin, and Waterford. Ignoring the terms of the treaty, *Strongbow* invaded Connaught in 1177, but was severely defeated by O'Connor in an epic battle.

The O'Brannains along with many other old Gaelic families was stripped of their lands and titles around this time. Some of the deposed O'Brannains formed together as bands of *Raparees* and *Tories* and many became highwaymen as a means of survival. One of the effects of this invasion by Henry II was that many of the old Gaelic names became anglicized. The name O'Brannain became Brennan. Some of these Brennans went on to become, quite famous in their time.[7]

---

[7] Fenlon, Donal, Royal Society of Antiquaries of Ireland. E-mail Interview. 14 Sept. 2011.

One notable was the Most Reverend John Brennan (1625-1693), Bishop of Waterford and Archbishop of Cashel. He was a friend of Geoffrey Keating who contributed to the writings in the *Book of Invasions*. He was also a close friend and confidante of Oliver Plunkett, the Bishop of Drogheda. His written reports to Rome were greatly valued by the historians in the 17th century, and still are today. He was subjected to the special attention of the *Priest Hunters*, yet he managed to elude them. (Maybe he had mastered the art of shape shifting as taught by the Druids). Oliver Plunkett was not as fortunate because Cromwell had him beheaded and his head put on a spike outside the Cathedral, as a deterrent to others.

Another John Brennan (1768-1830) was a noted doctor in Dublin. He became known affectionately as the *wrestling* doctor because if a patient could not pay his bill he had to take part in a wrestling match with him. He was also a writer and famous for his satires on the other doctors in Dublin, of his day. He is credited with being the chief of the Brennan clan at the time. Abbot Peter Brennan who lived in a monastery in France, having been sent into exile, was executed by guillotine in 1798 for his resistance to the French revolution.   Perhaps the most famous (or infamous), was William Brennan, highwayman extraordinaire, lovingly known as *Willie*. He was adept at relieving the Royal mail coaches of their spoils. In fact, he was so well known a song was written about him called *Brennan on the Moor* that is still sung in the hostelries around the world to this day. Many years later, James Freney, one of the most intrepid and some say chivalrous highwaymen (he was very polite when robbing his victims,) said that he had been instructed in this fine art by the Brennans. Then the authorities proceeded to hang him.

The Brennans

The First One

Ireland emerged slowly from the death grip of the last ice age around 10,000 years ago. The land bridges that connected it with its nearest neighbors, England and Scotland, vanished as the vast ice sheets melted. A tale is told of the arrival of Cessair, a daughter of Noah's son Bith and his wife Birren, just prior to the great deluge. She is said to be the first named individual to arrive in Ireland and was buried on the summit of Knockmaa, which is located southeast of Tuam, in county Galway.

Cessair did come with fifty men,

to County Cork one fine spring day.

The ice had gone from off the glen,

ten hundred years, now long astray.

The flood to flee and its huge swell,

no room upon the ark, they say.

Were kin of Noah, so they tell,

left Bith and Birren far away.

Sailed the seas for seven years,

a deluge would sweep all life away.

Heart sore, spent and full of fears,

a green land beckons, this fine day.

A land of mists and young oak tree,

with lake and hill in future time.

Fleet fawns wild, and running free,

it is empty now, but soon will shine.

Some will take it, as if their own,

others more kind and loving be.

More will raze it down and burn,

the deaf ear hard, the eye not see.

John A. Brennan

CHAPTER 2

The Turning Point

Europe, in the middle of the 5th century AD, was in darkness and fear was dominant. The Master (the druid) sensed fundamental change. A new religion was upon him and his people.

The Master

In the cool of early evening, they would gather in the grove, beneath the sheltering embrace of the sacred white oak tree. The Master had carefully dowsed the area, and had chosen it for the serene beauty and peaceful aura. The salmon-filled, clear waters of the river wound a course through the center as it made the long journey to its birthplace, the sea. They met there every year at the edge of twilight on the last day in October, to thank their ancestors, the providers, for their bounty. They referred to this day as Samhain, the end of summer and the eve of the New Year. The gentle breeze wafting through the dying leaves caused the long shadows to flit and dance, as if eager to join with them in their joyous celebration.

Waiting for him, they reflected on the year that had just passed. It had been fruitful, the crop yields being more abundant than usual. The plantings had germinated earlier than expected, and the oats and barley seemed to have been pushed upward from mother earth by a loving, enthusiastic, unseen hand. The children, ruddy cheeked, were vigorous and never happier.

The Master had said that they needed to grow faster now, and had cast many spells over their heads. There were those among them who swore that they could see and hear the growth, and would look at each other knowingly. The livestock were healthy, and many young had been born in the spring. Several sets of twins had been produced that year too. It was a good time to be alive and feel a part of it all. Not even the rumors of the foreigners in the land to the east worried them. They had heard of the slaughter on the other island and many were frightened. Yet Master assured them no harm would come to them.

For centuries, the tribes had managed to keep one-step ahead of the violent legions by moving swiftly, always at night. He had taught them how to shape shift and blend in with their surroundings. Eventually they made their final stand on the rocky, windswept Isle of Angle that lay off the coast of the Welsh lands. Some of them fled to the highlands in the north hoping for refuge there. Others stayed and fought, even though he had advised against it, there being too many of the enemy. Now as they advanced, he assembled his people and advised that they set sail as quickly as possible. Working together, they gathered the ash and birch saplings, the hides of their sacrificed animals, and built the Curraghs, the small boats that would bring them to the new land. They were grateful to him for his guidance and strength, as he saved them once again. Then, bidding farewell to their brothers, and with no fear, they cast off into the open sea, tacked west, and sailed out into the unknown.

Now in the new land, rumors were spreading of a lone stranger landing on their shores to the north, speaking in a strange language about new things. The Master had heard that he had gone to a rowan tree and cut a staff from it. The Master knew of this stranger and understood he would have to face him soon. He did not fear the violent strangers to the east but this lone figure scared him with his other worldly knowledge. Until now, he had guided his people in all things, the best time to plant, when to reap, what herbs to use to cure illness. He was the teacher and knew all and when they had doubts and fears he reassured them, without him they would be lost.

His lineage stretched back for eons and the secrets were passed down orally to him as they had always been. No written records were kept for fear of them falling into the wrong hands and being misused. But now he felt threatened. What was he to do? As his people stood there in the glade waiting, their robes fluttering in the soft evening breeze, they believed all would be well. This new land had many forests teeming with fallow deer and provided them with timber, meat, and hides. The diverse species of trees were revered by all for their magical powers and the fruits they bore. The oak was the king and his fruit, the acorn, was particularly prized.

They had watched as he dropped small berries from the hazel tree in the river and wait for the Salmon to surface and eat of them.   They were amazed as they observed him deftly grasp the swift, slippery fish directly from the rippling waters, eat the raw flesh to gain the ancient knowledge, then share it with them. The rowan was a powerful tree as well and he always cut from its thick inner growth, a staff and a dowsing rod, the symbols of his power. From the elder and blackthorns he taught them how to brew elixirs using the ripe berries mixed with the sweet honey from the bees. He had shown them how to make a potion from the leaves and berries of the mistletoe and then feed it to the animals in the rutting season. This would ensure vigorous and abundant offspring. Now, as they waited, they hoped he would come soon, so that the celebrations could begin.

Earlier in the year, on a warm summer afternoon, the Master, beset with feelings of unease and worrisome thoughts, had retreated to the forest. He sat alone at the mouth of the black cave deep in contemplation, his purple robes, and long red cloak fastened about his neck with a golden clasp. His long hair and beard were silvery as a moon's glow and neatly combed. His brow, deeply etched, spoke of the many years of worry endured on behalf of his beloved people, but his bright blue eyes were clear and focused. His sturdy staff rested on a moss covered rock by his side. As he sat, he read again, the old Oagham inscriptions, which were cut into the outer cave wall. He had added his own over the years, using a sharpened piece of flint. The carvings always gave him inspiration in times of doubt, and he had doubts now. So many relied on him alone that his broad shoulders sagged slightly as he worried about what was to come.

He always entered the silent realm when vital decisions had to be made. As he pondered, the veil slowly parted and he was granted a vision. With piercing clarity, he could see a robed stranger standing on a pebbled beach, on the northern shore. In his right hand, he held a staff with a crooked top. A deep sense of foreboding swept over him then, like a cold ocean wave, and soon he was awash with dark, dreadful thoughts of self-doubt and insecurity. This stranger had come, not with an army but with symbols more powerful. What was he to do? He had heard that the stranger had been here once before as a boy, taken by a raiding party from his home in the land to the East and had lived as a sheepherder on the slopes of Slemish, the fiery mountain. But that was many years ago, and the boy had since returned to his own people across the sea. Now he had come back. Why? What did it mean?

After consulting with the yellow robed lawmakers, the Brehons, and telling them of his vision, he had asked for their advice. They listened intently and advised him to make the journey to Tara, and meet again with them there. He set off early on the appointed morning, before the dew had dried off the grasses. At the top of the low hill above the river, he glanced over his shoulder, and directed his gaze toward the village in the valley below. The clay and wattle built dwellings were quiet, smoke from the peat fires curled upward and mingled with the fading mist, all was peaceful. Satisfied, he then turned his footsteps toward the west, and began his journey. The trek to the sacred mound at *Bru Na Boine* took two days to complete.

After placing his offerings in the inner chamber there, he continued further westward along the river, to the ring fort on the hill. There, king Laoghaire and the Brehons were waiting. He smiled, recalling his last visit when he had attended this new king's coronation. As he approached the ramparts, he was met by the ever-alert gatekeepers, and after crossing the deep earthen ditch, was escorted inside the walled enclosure. A sense of humility descended upon him then and he immediately felt the serenity of oneness. Once inside the great hall he had stood with head bowed, and waited.

He knew that his people were waiting patiently for him, but first he had something more important to do. As he sat outside the cave once more, on the eve of Samhain, his mind returned to Tara and the advice given him there. He would heed their advice as always, but before doing so he would consult the ancestors again, just to be sure. He reached into the deerskin pouch that hung about his waist and brought out the small, inscribed stones from within.

There were seven in number, and had been passed down to him by his father many years ago. As he shook them in his loosely cupped hands, he chanted the spells that would invoke the wisdom of the ancients, and cast them on the ground. Bending over to read, he noticed the dark eyed, dappled fawn emerge from the cool forest, and after passing through a patch of fading sunlight, approach him unafraid. This was not unusual. As she came closer and nestled at his feet, he reached out to her. It was as if to greet an old friend. As he stroked the silken fur on her breast, gently, she licked his hand. At that moment, a wren lit on the branches of a small blackthorn tree nearby, and sang her song for him. He smiled then knowing what he must do. Another glance at the stones confirmed his belief, and picking them up, returned them safely to their resting place. He then rose to go to his people, tell them of his decision, and fulfill his destiny with no regrets.

The Desert Monks.

Bob Marley once told me *"Every conversation be a revelation."* How very profound and true that would turn out to be, at least in my case. A casual meeting with a stranger on a river many years later brought Bob's words back to me and started me on a journey that is still ongoing. On a fascinating trip down the Nile to visit the temples at Abu Simbel, I fell into conversation with a fellow traveler, who like me was in search of ancient history and knowledge. We were discussing the role of scribes in Egypt and the wonderful way that they used Hieroglyphics as a form of written language. I have always been fascinated by the distinct connection between Egypt and Ireland and had read that a visit to Ireland by seven desert monks in the 8th Century AD is mentioned in the litany of Irish saints.

The first monk, Anthony of Egypt is depicted in carvings on many of the Irish high crosses. We went on to talk about the Irish monks who had done the same thing by recording history with their Oagham and Gaelic scripts. That meeting sparked my curiosity and re-lit the fire for me. When I returned home, I researched the history a little deeper.

As I delved into the far reaches of the shrouded history, one persistent thought kept crossing my mind. *Writing is the key to it all.*

I discovered that Monasticism developed in Egypt during the 3rd. Century AD. Most of the ascetics during that period of history lived solitary lives. They were called hermits, and they lived in simple huts or caves. One of these hermits was a man named Pachomius who was born in Thebes, modern day Luxor, in 292 AD to pagan parents. He was drafted into the Roman army against his will, at age 20 and held captive. He writes that local Christians, at great risk to themselves, brought food and water to the captives and these acts of kindness made a lasting impression on him. For Pachomius, that was the spark. When he was finally released, he sought out the hermit Palaemon and became his follower. Earlier, an ascetic named Anthony, who was born around 250 AD, had decided to retreat from society and devote himself to a solitary, contemplative life.[8]

After Anthony's parents died, he gave away his inheritance and went to live in an abandoned fort in the desert between the Nile and the Red sea and for twenty years saw no other human. Soon, others inspired by his lifestyle became followers and set up simple stone shelters around the fort. These small structures were called *cells*. Pachomius later took the next logical step and grouped these *cells* into a formal organization. In this way the first monastery was born. He knew instinctively that oral knowledge could easily be lost and so *insisted* his followers become *fully* literate. This would insure that as much information as possible could be saved if written down. Pachomius was hailed as *Abba*, which means father, and from this, we get the word Abbot.

---

[8] "Monasticism." *Wikipedia: The Free Encyclopedia*. Wikimedia Foundation Inc., 17 Feb. 2014. Web. 10 Mar. 2012.

Before I go any further, I feel that it is extremely important now, to write a little about the invaluable role the female followers played during this period. While perhaps not as well remembered as their male counterparts, they are nevertheless, a vital part of this story. Without their support and equal dedication, it is unlikely that the work of the males would have been as successful as it has been. Mary, Pachomius' sister, had lived in a cave near to him and gathered, over time, a group of other women who became the first, all female monastics. These women were adept at illustrating manuscripts as well as drawing detailed sketches for the architects who would eventually build the monasteries. They also wove the tapestries that adorned the walls and made the exquisite robes worn by the clergy. Reading and writing were taught by these women as well as many forms of art.

Basil the Great was born in Cappadocia around 330AD into a wealthy and influential family. He is arguably the most influential of the Greek monks. It appears that he was greatly influenced by his sister Macrina. As a young man, Basil sought to become a lawyer; however, he was persuaded by his sister to follow a more spiritual path. After a visit to Egypt, he decided to found his own monastery. He went on to write *The Monastic Rule*, which is still adhered to, by the Greek and Slavonic churches today

Brigit is arguably the most influential of the female monastics. She was born in County Louth. Ireland in 453 AD. Her father is believed to have been a pagan Chieftain of Leinster and her mother a Christian Pict and slave whom St. Patrick had baptized. She built a small oratory in County Kildare, which was a center of religion, and learning that eventually became a Cathedral city. She also founded two monastic institutions, one for men, and the other for women. She also founded a school of art, including illumination, metalwork and a scriptorium.

If any of those brilliant, far sighted individuals were to come back to this mortal realm, if just for one day, I would ask each of them one question. "Do you have any regrets with what you set out to accomplish?" I am certain that their voices in unison would reply loudly "No, no regrets."

5th Century Monasticism.
Photo appears courtesy of D.P. Walker and istockphoto.com

Historical place of worship
Photo courtesy of Pixabay Images

The Scribes

In 406AD during a particularly harsh winter, the river Rhine froze over. Across this temporary land bridge poured hordes of Germanic tribes led by the charismatic king of the Visigoths, Aleric. This singular event precipitated the fall of the mighty Roman Empire. The Empire began when a group of Latin speaking farmers made the life changing decision to settle in one place and leave the nomadic lifestyle behind. As their numbers grew, more land was needed for agriculture and thus the Empire grew. Ironically, it would be overwhelmed by much the same forces that had created it. The Empire fell exactly as foretold in the prophecy of the *Twelve Eagles, which* claimed that Rome would last twelve centuries and then fall. When the Germanic tribes invaded the Roman homelands, the *dark ages* began.

With the fall, Europe descended into chaos and darkness. All scholarship ceased, books were burned and learned men were rounded up, imprisoned and executed; the blackboard was being erased. Ireland, being an insular island, escaped all of this mayhem and actually blossomed intellectually during this period, due in large part to the foresight, dedication, and tenacity of a handful of scholar monks. Those brave men travelled everywhere across the then, known world, and collected as much of the written history that had not already been destroyed. They brought the written words back to Ireland and passed them on to their brothers, the scribes. [9]

If I close my eyes and am very still, I can conjure up the vision of a monk alone in his cold, stone cell, isolated in a dark monastery. I can imagine, the silence shrouding him as he pored over those ancient scrolls by

---

[9] Ibid.

candlelight, his eyes bright with wonder. Then, word for word, reveal, translate and write down with a quill he fashioned from a reed, or perhaps a goose feather and ink that he himself blended. In the deep silence, you would hear the scratch of the nib as he wrote on the stiff parchment. For him, at that time, it must have been a sacred and painstaking task. It amazes me when I think of the time, patience and dedication those men had in order to ensure that future generations would come to know and marvel at their revelations. For the most part, they were of good cheer and never lost their sense of humor.

If you look closely at any of their works, you will notice, in the margins, their scribbled jokes, usually at the expense of a fellow scribe. I have often wondered where those monks got their knowledge of the Greek, Hebrew and Latin languages and the ability to translate them, this being an era when all formal education had been eradicated. I have pondered this for the longest time and an odd idea kept crossing my mind.

What if a particular man from Galilee really was who he claimed to be? What if everything that has been said about him is true? Could he really have instilled in his disciples the supernatural ability to speak and understand all tongues, then send them forth to teach whomever they encountered? If so, for me that would explain the tireless drive and commitment of those monks.

In the final analysis, to all of them we owe a huge debt. The most fitting way to repay their sacrifice is for us to follow their example and just keep on writing and in so doing make a difference in the world. In this way will we be able to stave off any potential regrets we may have later on in our lives.

John A. Brennan

In My Blood

Must I bleed all over the page
and purge my soul for all to see?
Rend open wide the deep dark rage,
will I then regain my sanity?
The mind in a whirl and racing
like a heartbeat bursting free.
Expel the thoughts, pain embracing
when once a story comes to be.
Can these words fulfill my need
or uncoil the depths of disparity?
Or bind me fast on endless seas
with roiling thoughts and fantasy.
Blood must spill across the page
or else coagulation rules.
If not expressed, this hidden rage
will blind and smite us all as fools.
Once heart's blood has, poured, clear through
relief will come and pain abate.
Released from fear if what I do,
is tell the tale with honest faith.

Back When

Oh to return to that time, place and space of yesterday's papers. Back when I was young, undaunted, and sure of nothing. When I was stronger than an oak. Spellbound in innocence.

Back when Joe Cocker sang about too many lovers and not
enough love, thanks Joe...thanks for nothing.
What did he know with his tortured soul flailing and
stripped bare as a tree in winter. Back when war was the ever-present companion.

Back when the FBI and the CIA and the IRA and the BBC and the fingerprint files crowded and smothered the senses. Back when blood flowed crimson down the streets of my town. Congealed and then stained the Holy ground.

Front Cover: Ireland's Dunluce Castle Co. Antrim Northern Ireland.
Photo appears courtesy of K-Stuart and Istockphoto.com.

CHAPTER 3

The Connection

For as long as I can remember, I have had a burning desire to see as many of the ancient sacred places in this world. To try to understand how and why each one of them is connected, find the common thread, you might say. I believe that when people die they do not just disappear. I like to think of them as having ascended. I am convinced that they continue to affect us in our world and are all around us. Their essence is almost tangible and their energy seems, at least to me, to be very powerful. You will experience those feelings anytime you enter a quiet, empty house of worship, the particular denomination does not matter. Or visit, as I have, any of the ancient, sacred sites. The silence and stillness are what strike you first. You will feel instinctively, that there is a benign presence surrounding you.

Without exception, the sense of awe, humility and wonderment were exactly the same when I climbed to the top of Machu Pichu in the highlands of Peru, or when I descended into the Queen's chamber in the heart of the Great Pyramid at Giza. When I walked along the Avenue of the Dead in Teotihuacan taouachan, Mexico, I marveled at the beauty and the incredible detail of the ancient Pyramids of the Sun and Moon. As I was lying in a hammock, listening to the silence of the night in the jungle in Ecuador, a feeling of oneness came over me. Moreover, just standing at a simple Mass Rock in Ireland conveys that it is all a continuum. There is a profound sense of the sacred that unites each one of these places, and I believe that it can be absorbed and utilized.

I am sure that this desire started in one distinct area of Ireland, where, as a child, I spent my formative years. This area is known as the parish of *Upper Creggan*. Annamar, *black Castle*, is a court cairn tomb built in the Mesolithic age. The work was completed around 2800BC. It is believed to be one of a series of passage graves that have endured. Many still dot the landscape of Ireland today. I lived as a one year old with my parents in a small rented cottage close to this court cairn, for about a year. As a child, I absorbed the energy that emanated from those ancient stones. Ever since then, I have been drawn to all sacred sites, which although built of rough stone, were erected with such precision, both mathematically and astronomically, they defy our understanding.

When I was two years old, we moved to live in an old two-storied house in Urker, a mile or so outside the town of Crossmaglen, County Armagh. The name Urker translates as, *to cast or throw* and according to the historian, Hugh Macauley, it is likely that the name derives from an old funerary practice of mourners *casting* stones to form a cairn on or near a grave, an ancient headstone, if you like. I lived in Urker until I was nine years old. Close to the house where we lived was a *Mass Rock*. These rocks date from a dark era in Irish history and it always drew my attention. I write more about them in a later chapter. [10]

If you are of an open mind and believe that truly, everything *is* possible, then you will find that we interact with the ascended on a regular basis, knowingly or not. Think of the many times in your life when you felt

---

[10] McShane, Michael. *"Artificial Curiosities and Antiquities of the South Armagh Countryside."* Journal of Creggan Local History. Creggan History Society. Society, 28 12 2008. Web. Mar 2011.

that light tap on your shoulder, only to turn around and there is no one there. Or the times when you could have sworn you heard someone call your name, clearly and distinctly, only to discover that you are quite alone. Maybe you were not…

My Grandfather

My grandfather, Jack Brennan, ascended when I was seven years old and I was there at the exact moment that he left this earth. Friends and neighbors had gathered and knelt by his bedside to pray and bid him au revoir. He was stretched out on his bed upstairs in the middle room of my Uncle Joe's house in 18 Rathview park. We lived in the old two storied, rented house in Urker and my mother and I walked hand in hand, into the town to see him for the last time. He was a tall man, in his eighties, with a shock of gray hair and I clearly remember him motioning for me to come nearer. As I did, he took my hand and smiled. He held it in a tight grip for what seemed an eternity. I felt a burning sensation as the heat from his hand traveled up my right arm and spread throughout my entire body. He expired right at that moment. My mother had to pry his fingers open to extract my hand from his. My father explained to me later that my grandfather was passing his power and knowledge on to me. I heard stories about him over the years and all I can say about him is that he was widely known and highly respected for his fairness and integrity. He hated injustice, naysayers and always favored the underdog. If he saw two men gang up on one, he would even the odds by pulling one of them out of the fray.

The Apparition

It was Samhain, the night of the Celtic New Year. The night when the veil between worlds was parted. The night when the spirits could commune with earthly mortals. As a child, he had often heard the tales told around the fireside but as he grew older, he dismissed them as harmless ghost stories.

As the fog rolled slowly over the dark, empty, expansive square, it blanketed everything and clung with damp tenacity. He walked a diagonal path with assured steps, toward home, coat buttoned all the way up, both hands buried deep in the pockets, hat pulled down tightly on his head. The echo of his footsteps, muffled by the slowly thickening mist, could still be heard and made for an oddly comforting companion as he went along. He was late and knew some explaining would have to be done. He also knew that Mary would understand and be forgiving as always. The quietness was made all the more complete as the mist got denser. It was four in the morning, the time when the body's defenses are at their lowest ebb. The card game had not gone well, but then that was nothing new. He was lucky in other areas, but not cards. The two glasses of strong whisky he had savored earlier came to his aid now and formed a warm envelope against the early morning chill. *Thank God for the illicit distillers,* he mused, laughing softly. He would have to quit playing cards he resolved, for the umpteenth time. As he walked along peering into the darkness ahead, he suddenly felt as if he was slowing down, as if he was pushing against an invisible force. *That cannot be,* he reasoned, and stopped walking.

Usually, not a fearful man, now, a chill ran down his spine and he suddenly felt afraid. As he looked ahead once more, he could see a form taking shape, human in appearance. Averting his eyes, he changed direction and tried to walk faster. But no matter how hard he tried, he made no headway. It felt like he was frozen to the spot. Daring to look ahead again, he saw that the form was still in front of him. In desperation, he tried again to move, but was unable to. No matter which way he turned, the form, now distinctly human, was always in front of him. In a hoarse whisper, he called out, "Who's there?"

Shocked by the tremor in his usually firm voice he waited. There was no answer. At that moment, he made the sign of the cross and, although not a very religious man, said a prayer. He felt icy cold now and sweated with abject fear. He looked around trying to get his bearings but the mist had grown denser and he could see little more than arm's length. A looming darkness descended, slowly forming a cocoon around his trembling body, cloaking him with invisible completeness.

In a choked whisper he asked, "What do you want with me?" His mind racing, he shut his eyes and waited for an answer. For what seemed an eternity, he stood immobile. When he dared, he slowly opened his eyes and discovered that the fog and the specter had gone. Glancing around, he gasped when he saw that he was inches away from the open mouth of the old water well. As he looked, he saw that the wooden cover was missing. Relief soon replaced his fear and he nervously continued on his way toward home, his footsteps faltering. When he arrived home, the house was quiet. Mary, his wife, was asleep. Shaken, and still trying to make sense of what had happened, he began to prepare for bed. When he looked in the mirror, he was further shocked to see that his hair had turned white!

Later that morning, he was roused from a fitful sleep by someone shaking him. As he turned over, his eyes focused and he saw Mary standing at the bedside with her hand covering her mouth. "God save us, Jack Brennan! What happened? You look like you've seen a ghost!" He touched his head with trembling fingers and asked, his voice quavering, "Is it still white? I hoped it was all just a horrible dream." He never drank liquor or played cards again after the night of that otherworldly encounter.

Jack said many years later that the fright he got on the square that foggy, dark night was the best thing ever happened to him. When asked to explain what he meant he replied, "It all made me think about the direction my life was going. After I stopped drinking and gambling my life took a favorable turn, I was able to think more clearly and focus on the important things. If I hadn't had that encounter I would have carried on as I was doing and probably ended up with many regrets. Now, I tell my children often, whatever they do in life, *"**don't die with regrets.**"*

Jack Brennan (1949)

The Escape

He'd had a narrow escape the day before. They had almost caught him and he was lucky that he managed to elude them. An icy cold sweat broke out on his furrowed brow as he remembered it. He had started out just as the sun rose above the copse that surrounded his small, lime washed, thatched cottage at the top end of the town. After dressing in silence, he stoked the fire, hung the kettle on the chimney hook, over the flames, and as it boiled, readied his mug. Glancing in the mirror to straighten his hat and tie, two clear blue eyes looked back at him and chuckling he thought, *you will do*. He had shaved the night before knowing it would give him more time in the morning. Placing several bricks of peat on the dying embers in the open hearth, he drained his mug and stepped outside.
Breathing deeply, savoring the clear, crisp morning air, he made his way to the stable where he kept his pride and joy, and only means of transport.

He could hear her neighing softly in recognition, and the clop of her hooves as she came towards the door to greet him. Stepping inside he inhaled the earthy smell of hay and oats mixed with the strong aroma of horse. He was met with a wet nuzzle and felt all would be well. Taking the nosebag from the hook on the wall beside the door, he filled it with a mixture of oats and barley from the oak barrel and hung it loosely around her head. He loved the new mare, she was fast and responded to his every command with a willingness he had coaxed from her with gentle murmurs and whispers over a period of time. Mary, his wife, had joked more than once that he thought more of the horse than he did of her.

Sadness swept over him like a cold ocean wave when the old mare died, and he felt that he would never replace her with one as good. Now, he smiled as he remembered the day that he found the new one. One spring

morning he attended the fair held on the large, open square every first
Friday of every month. After a lot of haggling and hand slapping he bought
her from a roving gypsy, who assured him that if it wasn't for his starving
children, and the pocket paralysis that beset him at that moment, he would
never part with her. Telling the story later he recalled with a grin, "The
gypsy man was so heartbroken to see her go, he went straight to the nearest
bar to drown his sorrows."

He had an affinity with all animals and often said that he preferred
them to some of the humans he knew. With the mare munching
contentedly, he reached over to the shelf and picked up the currycomb and
stiff brush. "Good girl," he murmured softly as he began to brush her with
loving, delicate strokes. "We have a job to do today, girl. How are those
new shoes, do they feel alright?" He had asked Kelly the blacksmith, to
fashion a pair of lightweight horseshoes for her and had them fitted a week
earlier. She definitely seemed lighter on her feet and could run faster than
before. *We may need all the speed we can get before this day is over*, he thought,
ruefully. With her coat a glossy black sheen, he stepped outside and walked
the few paces to the well, dropped the bucket inside and waited until he
heard the familiar splash as it hit the surface of the water.

As he hauled the bucket up the well shaft, he thought of the day he
bought the cottage, and how the well had been one of the greatest selling
points for him. Pouring the fresh water in the trough, which sat just inside
the stable door against the left sidewall, he reached over with one hand, and
removed the now empty nosebag and set it on top of the oak barrel. He
walked to the shed opposite, swung open the double doors, went inside,
and took hold of one of the shafts of his cart. Pulling it into the yard, the
metal wheel rims crunched on the graveled surface, startling several
watchful crows who, with angry *caws* took flight from their perches, high up

in the old hazel tree at the roadside. He did not like crows and thought them bad omens.

Placing the collar and the bitless bridle around the mare's neck, he guided her in between the shafts, then, coupled the straps to the rings. He refused to put a *bit* in her mouth as he considered them a cruel invention that made the horse suffer needlessly. He believed that if treated with care and attention any horse could be directed solely with gentle tugs on the reins. Filling the nosebag once more, he tied the neck shut and placed in in the cart under the seat. He returned to the shed, walked to the back wall, and removed a short, loose board. Reaching inside, his hand closed around a small, canvas wrapped bundle, which he immediately slipped into his coat pocket. After replacing the board, he went outside and closed the doors. One last look around assured him that all was as should be.

By then, the sun had climbed higher in the cloudless sky, bathing them with a warm glow and it looked like it would be a good day. The sound of a thrush warbling her morning song from atop a whitethorn tree held his attention for a while. Climbing up onto the cart seat he whispered a silent prayer that all would go well. As he cracked the whip lightly above her head, the mare started moving slowly forward. Off in the distance he could see that the mist on the slopes of Slieve Gullion, the flat topped, extinct, volcanic mountain with the lake on the summit, was almost gone, and he felt better. He had made this trip many times before and knew the risks involved but had to make the choice knowing that his family had to be supported at all costs. Ireland in the mid-1920s was a tough place to live. He had to supplement his meager earnings somehow and knew of no other way than this. The bloody civil war, which started soon after the War of Independence ended, lasted for almost a year and divided former comrades and indeed whole families, as sides were chosen in the conflict. The civil war ended in May 1923 and it was then that the country was divided. A borderline on the map annexed the six northern counties from the rest of the island. From the start, he had been against the wretched treaty that the Irish Republican Army had signed with England at the end of the war of Independence. He knew that the nationalist population would be the minority then and completely at the mercy of the loyalists. Families that still considered themselves purely Irish by birth found themselves living in the British controlled area of the so-called, Northern Ireland state, separate and distinct from the rest of the island. Michael Collins, who was the negotiator on the Irish side, later said that in signing the treaty he had signed his own death warrant. This was prophetic, as not long after he was killed in an ambush in County Cork, by his former compatriots.

It had already started to turn for the worse with most of the jobs going to the Loyalists. Catholics were not allowed to vote, and housing was almost non-existent. The pogroms had already started in several areas of Belfast. They were dark and frightening times. Thankfully, Frank Aiken still maintained his northern, *flying column*. He would be there if needed to protect the catholic population. Aiken was insistent that Catholics arm themselves for safety. We need more men like Frank, he thought and laughed silently at the irony of the completely sickening mess. What the British failed to realize was that the drawing of the border had unearthed an otherwise non-existent opportunity for him and others who were brave or foolish enough to run the gauntlet.

With the disparity that existed between the two currencies, goods bought south of the border could now be sold for a small profit on the northern side. How strange, he thought, that history does indeed repeat itself and he recalled the story his father had told him about the displacement of his ancestors by the Norman invaders in the 1100s. Some of them became highwaymen and regularly robbed the British mail coaches, partly in retribution but mostly as a way to survive. They even wrote a song about the exploits of one of the more famous, or infamous one, titled *Brennan on the moor.* He had heard his father sing it many times and sang it himself on occasion. He did not feel much like singing now though, maybe later if he got home safely. Pulling back on the reins, the mare slowed and came to a stop. Taking a long a swig from the bottle he had placed under the cart seat the night before, he waited for the familiar warm glow, then moved forward once more.

They met no one on the road south toward the border and as they passed Lough Ross he shook his head from side to side grinning wryly as he thought, *fishing will never be the same again.* The borderline cut invisibly across the fields and the lake, leaving one-half in the Irish Republic and the other half in the Northern State. *Maybe I could catch fish in the south and sell them in the north for a profit. Would the southern fish have an accent? Would the northern fish have to swear allegiance? Or would cows that ate grass on the southern end of a field have to pay duty on their milk if sold in the north?* He laughed again silently at his own jokes. All of these questions because of that Collins fella. *He should have held out for total freedom.* Shaking off the annoying reverie, he noticed that he was almost at the border, the only visible evidence a large yellow sign that read in large, forbidding letters *Unapproved Road.* He stopped and looked all around taking in the hedgerows and fields. All seemed quiet with no one else in sight, but you never knew.

Here we go, he thought and with a sharp snap of the reins, they moved off again, and crossed the invisible borderline.

They made good time and soon he could see the spire nestled atop the bell tower of the little church in the distance, and knew that they would arrive in the small market town in ten more minutes. He decided to go straight to the poultry market on the other side of the town and not make any stops. Best to keep it simple, he thought. He pulled back slowly on the reins as they came to the corner where the poultry pens sat stacked neatly in rows and said, "good afternoon," to the owner, a red faced, good natured soul that he knew well.

"And the same to you John, any trouble coming down?"

"No trouble Jim, it's going back that I'm worried about."

"Did you get the new shoes we talked about the last time?"

"Yes, I had her fitted last week. James Kelly made them for me."

Kelly's forebears had been blacksmiths, and had made the pikes for the 1798 rebellion. He was not shy about telling you that fact or anyone else who would listen.

"Well then you have nothing to worry about, Kelly is the best blacksmith north or south. If they spot you she'll outrun them with ease."

"I hope so, Kelly said the same thing."

As they talked, he retrieved the nosebag and let the mare eat again.

"How many do you want today?"

"That all depends on the price."

"Six pounds for a dozen and that's a great bargain."

" Sure, it's a great bargain all right, for you Jim."

"You're a hard man to deal with John," he replied laughing.

"I'll give you three pounds."

"Aw, come on now John that's too little. Make it five."

"That's daylight robbery Jim, best I can do is four and you load them."

"You're the hardest man I ever dealt with, John."

" Tell you what I'll do, eight pounds for two dozen. You know that I will be back for more, god willing."

Then, with a loud slap of hands, the bargain was struck. Soon six small wire cages containing clucking chickens were placed in the back of the cart and readied for the journey north. Both men spread a large cover made of several jute bags sewn together, across the cages. "That will keep them quiet John." "Yes it will and away from prying eyes too."

Reaching under the seat he felt around for the bottle, finding it, he brought it out and called,

"Jim, I have something for you."

Keeping it under his coat, he waited for Jim to get close and then slipped it to him quickly. "Is this what I think it is?" The men exchanged knowing glances and nodded their heads.

" Have one for the road, John."

"Maybe I will," he said and jumped back down off the cart.

They went inside and once out of sight two short glasses were produced. Jim held the bottle up to the light and said,

"Clear as crystal, this is the good stuff."

Uncorking the bottle, he poured two healthy drinks of the illicit nectar. This was the homemade drink of choice for the discerning Irishman.

"Slainte John."

"Your health, Jim." Kelly reached into the inside pocket of his coat and brought out a sealed, long brown envelope and handed it to John. "Here, before I forget. If you run into any trouble make sure you burn this."

With that, the glasses were emptied and after a sharp salute, John started out on the return journey. *One more stop girl and then we will head home.*

Two miles outside the town, he pulled gently on the reins and stopped beside a small, two roomed, ivy covered cottage, which sat back off the roadside, and whistled twice. Immediately, two men wearing long, trench coats, collars turned up, their faces obscured by large, broad brimmed fedoras, came outside, and approached him hurriedly. Each man wore a wide leather belt around his waist, to which was attached a brown leather holster. A third man dressed identically, stood at the ready in the shadows of the open doorway, cradling a Thompson machine gun, unmoving. The two men were each carrying a grey woolen blanket tied securely at both ends and the middle. Ever watchful, and with furtive glances all around, they placed them in the concealed compartment under the body of the cart and slid the bolt shut. A sharp salute, then all three men disappeared back inside the cottage with not a word spoken.

A knot was forming in the pit of his stomach as he again neared the border and with twilight dropping slowly, he pulled back on the reins. "Whoa, girl," he said in a low voice.
The mare, obeying his command stopped and stood perfectly still, waiting. His eyes, ever alert, cast slow, piercing glances across the landscape missing no detail. He noticed the birds nesting in the hedgerows warbling their evening song and the cows in the fields lazily chewing.

He saw the sheep lying at ease in the lush meadow on the other side of the road. His gaze turned upward and watched as a small flock of rooks completed their approach and settled in the sprawling branches of a white oak tree. *Ahh... home for the night.* All was serene; nothing seemed out of place. Directing his gaze forward once more he peered off into the distance and could see the town on the hill, two miles away, *his town, his home.* As darkness descended, he saw that the lamps were slowly being lit, one by one. It was time to go. A couple of loud clicks of his tongue, a gentle snap of the reins and they moved forward. Illuminated by the glow of soft moonlight, the ribbon of road stretched out before him. The rhythmic *clip clop* of the hooves the only sound in the still night air. His night vision was now fully adjusted to the darkness but his view of the town was temporarily obscured as the road dipped abruptly before rising to the brow of a low-lying hill. He stopped on the crest and ever wary, scanned the horizon. His sharp gaze noticed a familiar narrow laneway on his right with thick blackthorn hedges growing on both sides. He knew the owner of the house at the end of the lane and had availed of his hospitality on more than one occasion. On each of the two large stone pillars, a hinged wrought iron gate hung in the open position. Suddenly, a faint flicker of light about a half mile away, just beyond the crossroads, caught his attention. Rubbing his eyes, he looked again, nothing. *That is strange*. Knowing the area well, he was sure there were no houses on that stretch. *Maybe it's a will-o-the-wisp* he chuckled nervously, remembering stories he had heard his father tell him as a boy.

There it was again! This time there was no mistake. Two points of light, reminding him of a cat blinking its eyes, flickered twice and then abruptly stopped. From the opposite side of the road and about one hundred yards closer to where he sat, three more flickers. *Aha, you bastards, I see you. You've got the crossroads covered! Bloody customs men!* He dreaded them especially as he knew that they were conspiring with the police. His alternate routes cut off, he thought of the items concealed underneath the body of the cart and made an instant decision. Jumping off the cart, he took the reins and led the horse slightly past the gateway. Then with an experienced hand, backed the cart into the laneway, closed the gates and tied the reins to one of them. He hung the nosebag around the horses head and patting her softly on the neck leaned close and said,
"*Shhhhh*, now you be quiet girl."

The old, well-greased metal bolt slid back silently allowing him to retrieve the bundles hidden underneath. Looking all around once more he was satisfied it was safe to move them. Grasping the cords, he hefted the bundles onto his shoulder and walked toward the house at the end of the lane. As he neared the dwelling, he was comforted to see there was a light in one of the small windows. Tapping gently on the glass using a pre-arranged signal, he waited. Soon the curtain was drawn and a familiar face peered out. Instant recognition prompted the owner to open the door quickly. "Are they out again tonight John?" he whispered. "Yes they're out, damn them, at least two of them, one on either side of the crossroads." "Come on, follow me."

The two men walked quickly around to the back of the house and stopped outside a large hay barn. Inside were stored enough bales to last as fodder for the animals through the remaining months of the year. Once inside they wasted no time moving several bales from the front of the large stack. This revealed a 12'x12' compartment lined on three sides with wide wooden planks. A series of shelves on which lay more similar bundles, were attached to two of the walls. Several large boxes were stacked neatly in one corner, the stenciled markings denoting the contents. Pinned on the third wall was an old, torn and stained, tri-colored flag. Beneath the flag on six metal hooks hung broad brimmed, black fedoras. Below the hats on six more hooks hung heavy, olive-green trench coats. Both men stood to attention and facing the flag, saluted. After placing the bundles on a shelf, they returned the bales to their original position and walked back to the house in silence. Inside the two men sat hunched over a small wooden table. A well-polished oil lamp, suspended on a chain from a hook in the ceiling, hissed quietly, illuminating a small waterproof, much creased map that was spread out on the surface. On top of the map lay a Webley pistol, a small box of ammunition, and the sealed envelope.

"Better to leave these with me tonight John, safer."

"Yes I agree, we must be careful."

"Well, we can't afford you being arrested or, God forbid, shot. We've lost enough good men already."

" Don't worry, I have no intention of letting that happen."

" Have you anything else in the cart?"

" Yes, I have two dozen chickens."

" Ok, I'll give you a receipt for them. When they stop and search you, just say you bought them from me." Opening the drawer a receipt book and pen were taken out and placed on the table, then after putting the weapon and ammunition in the drawer, the map was folded and pushed to one side. "How much did you pay for the fowl?" "I gave Kelly eight pounds." Some quick calculations were done, the receipt handed over, which John slipped into his pocket. "What about the stuff in the barn?'

" Don't worry about that, I'll send for someone later tonight to take it over the fields. One way or another it will be in place for tomorrow night." After a handshake and salute, the men parted.

Walking slowly along the lane, John felt in his pocket for the receipt. Re-assured, he removed the nosebag, led the horse and cart out onto the road and climbed aboard. Breathing deeply and saying a silent prayer he clicked his tongue, snapped the reins lightly and they moved forward. Just before reaching the crossroads, a sudden movement caused him to look toward his right. The horse kept a steady pace and trotted forward slowly. When they came alongside a gated entrance to a field, he saw that the gate was opened inwards. Peering intently, John could see the silhouette of a large car parked just inside the opening facing the road and as the cart passed, he heard the car door closing. The crossroads now behind them, they moved forward at a leisurely pace. Crossing the low stone bridge that spanned a narrow, fast flowing stream, the growl of the car as its engine started prompted him to act quickly. Before the mare could react to the sudden noise, John tightened the reins and kept her head down, saying softly, "Whoa, take it easy girl."

Keeping pace with the cart, the car followed behind, its engine purring quietly in low gear. Further up the road he could see the other car moving slowly toward them. Unnerved, John did what he always did in tense situations, he whistled. A soft and airless melody at first, but as his courage took hold he recalled an old song he had often heard his father sing and soon the notes carried upward on the night air. Suddenly, the darkness was gone as the headlights on the car behind him were turned on. Gripping the reins tighter his eyes followed the long eerie shadow of the horse and cart as it moved along the road ahead of them. As the car in front crept nearer the sensation of being trapped heightened, but with stubbornness, he continued to whistle. Remembering what his father and others had often told him to do when in bad situations, he now put their advice to the test. *Don't panic, whatever you do. Take control of the situation. Let them come to you.*

With those thoughts guiding him, and still whistling he jumped from the cart, stood holding the reins, and waited. The second cars headlights turned on then bathing the whole area with sharp, blinding light and he instinctively lowered his head and closed his eyes. The mare stood still and unafraid, the dazzling lights seeming not to affect her. Both cars rolled slowly closer and then stopped. Sandwiched between the two vehicles he raised his head, opened his eyes, and looked over his shoulder just as the driver stepped from the vehicle. Looking forward, he could see two more figures emerge from the second car. As the three men got closer, he could see that two of them wore customs officer uniforms, the light reflecting off the peaks of their caps. The third wore the uniform of a police officer and a quick glance, revealed a holstered pistol on the belt around his waist. *Stay calm!*

"Is that you John?" asked one of the men

"Oh, it's John alright," the man behind him, said. "I'd know that ugly face anywhere," laughed the police officer. "You're out late tonight John." "Yes I am. The mare threw one of her shoes earlier, slowed me down a bit. My wife will kill me when I get home."

" Do you have anything to declare, John?"

" I have some fowl that I purchased earlier."

" Anything else?"

" No, just the fowl, that's all."

" Are you sure about that John, because if you have anything else, you will regret it?"

" I'm sure, lord knows I don't want to have any regrets."

" Then you won't object if we search you and the cart, will you."

" Not at all, search all you want."

Thinking that they would just search the main body of the cart, John was shocked when the police officer got on his knees, reached under, and slid the bolt on the compartment. As the hinged flap opened, a set of horseshoes, hammer, nails, and a small can of axle grease fell out onto the road. Laying on his back to get a better view, the officer searched the recess. Satisfied, he rose to his feet and as he angrily kicked the tin of grease said, "There's nothing there. Nothing at all." *How did he know about the compartment? That's the first time they've ever done that! Damn them; we'll have to change tactics again.*

The customs officers had already pulled the cover back revealing the wire cages. After counting the fowl, they replaced the cover. "Do you have a receipt for these?" As John reached for his pocket, the police officer stopped him saying, "Put your hands up John, I'm going to search you." Raising his arms above his head he stood as the officer searched his pockets. With his face inches from his, John looked unflinching, in the officers angry, steel blue eyes. The strong odor of alcohol on his breath felt sickeningly hot on Johns face. Finding the receipt, he handed it to one of the customs officers saying, "Make sure this is alright and be sure to check it thoroughly." Then turning to John said,

"We are watching you John, just remember that. We are keeping a close eye on you." *You'd better keep both eyes on me boy, because we're watching you too.*

Handing him the receipt the customs officer said,

"Everything seems to be in order here. We wish you goodnight." Gathering the horseshoes, nails, and grease can from the road, he placed them in the cart and climbed onto the seat once more. He clicked his tongue, snapped the reins and finally they were on their way. Relieved that the ordeal was over, he relaxed. Without a backward glance, he started to hum a favorite tune. As the mare trotted surefooted and steady, bringing them both safely toward home, the humming soon became a song.

"God save Ireland cried the heroes

God save Ireland cry them all. If on the battlefield we die

Or upon the scaffold high

God save the heroes one and all."

The Rapparee

In memory of my ancestor William Brennan (Brennan on the moor)
who chose to become a highwayman after his forebears were ousted
from their ancestral home in county Kilkenny, during the Norman
invasion of Ireland.

He rode from high to the valley floor,
then hid behind the rowan tree.
It was time to settle a deep-set score
and seek vengeance for his family.

They took the land they took their pride,
rode roughshod o'er the scattered bones.
With mace and mail from far and wide,
castles shook, to the bare keep stones.

But now midst leaves, and masked and still,
flintlock and cutlass tried and true.
A glossy mare to do his will
those in league, are now sure to rue.

Coach rims crunch on graveled base
two pairs snort, wild manes aquiver.
He spurs her on, now quick apace.
"Halt there coachman. Stand and deliver!"

John A. Brennan

Back When

Back when Bobby Sands starved to death in Long Kesh
prison camp, his fingernails blackened. His body consumed
from within. Skeletal remains a stark reminder of nine more
to follow his lead. Willing political pawns.

Back when Joe Doherty escaped to the sanctuary of Manhattan's
upper eastside, tended bar at the Carlow East, until the
canary sang his traitors song.

Back when Fergal was shot to death on a Sunday morning
after mass, another innocent slaughtered.
Back when one man one vote was still just a dream.
Back when the street fighting men were on fire.
The fighting ten from Crossmaglen, harried, hunted, revered

Pacifists turned reluctant, universal soldiers for the cause.
Back when Sunday was bloodied in Derry
Thirteen their number. Gone. Immortals now.
Back when the women caged in Armagh jail
were violated, invaded, and defiled.

CHAPTER 4

On Childhood

My Father

My father Mal, was the greatest and most powerful influence on me as a child. Things he instilled in me would have a lasting and profound effect on my life. Although I didn't realize it as it was happening, his influence has guided my footsteps subconsciously, and still does, even from beyond this earthly realm. He grew up in a small village in Ireland called Crossmaglen, County Armagh and Armagh city has the unique distinction of being the Ecclesiastical capital of Ireland and has two Cathedrals. It is also known fondly as the *orchard* county, so named for the profusion of fruit trees grown there. My father had twin brothers and two sisters. I was named after one of his brothers, Anthony, who died tragically at age 13. He and some of his friends were playing a dangerous game where they would leap from rooftop to rooftop. Anthony fell between two houses and landed in the space between, dying immediately.

In my fathers' time Crossmaglen had a population of perhaps one thousand and sat, just a mile inside the imaginary borderline drawn on the map by the British authorities after the civil war ended in 1922. This line was etched on the map with cold, calculated precision to ensure that the population within its bounds remained protestant by majority. This would ensure a loyalist vote in favor of the Unionist party who had sworn their allegiance to the English crown. The British forces occupied Crossmaglen from the moment the border was drawn as they were convinced that the inhabitants were anti British rule.

It had then and indeed still has, a reputation for being a hotbed of rebelliousness and complete dismissal of British authority.

Mal was not an overly voluble man. He was reserved in his way of speaking yet he managed to instill in me tacitly, all of the fundamental qualities that he believed I would need in life. He led by example. He *showed* me. He seemed to know things instinctively and had an unquenchable thirst for knowledge. He believed that it was the duty of every man to pass on all positive knowledge to everyone. Holding it back and keeping it to yourself, he believed, was self-centeredness and tantamount to disaster. He took things apart to understand better, how they worked and amazingly, could re-assemble them perfectly without the aid of manuals. Whether it was a clock that he felt ticked slower than it should or a motor bike that he felt was not *quite* right, it mattered little to him.

When we got our first television set, it too could not escape his ever curious mind. Convinced always that he could improve the reception, it was not unusual to find him up on the roof adjusting and re-adjusting the antenna. He was undaunted. He detested *naysayers* and the word *impossible* and was adamant that the word was only used by complainers and defeatists. A favorite expression of his was,
"Nothing is impossible! If you let *Impossible* into your life, you will most assuredly die with regrets!"

How did he know all of these things having only had a basic education? As I traced his lineage, I began to see more clearly the connection with his ancestors, his *people* as he called them. He believed that the skills which they possessed were passed on down through the generations and are in our genes. They are hardwired into our synapses. Knowledge is never lost, it is lodged in the collective subconscious waiting to be awakened and remembered. An example of this illustrates this fact perfectly. Did you ever awake from a dream, but could not recall all of the details? Next time, upon waking, write down any part you recall no matter if it's only one or two words and set it aside with the intention of glancing at it later in the day. You will find more often than not that you will recall more details and eventually the dream will slowly unravel in your conscious mind. The following short stories hopefully capture my father's essence. Enjoy!

The Rock

A lesson on History

It looked sad and forlorn sitting by the side of the Creamery road as though it knew that it had long been abandoned. I first noticed it one rainy afternoon when I was almost seven years old. I can still vividly recall the sweet scent of wild honeysuckle, hanging heavily on the air that day. At first glance, it was just another large, almost perfect, square shaped rock, covered with briars and moss, but there was an almost eerie attraction to it as if it wanted to tell me something. I didn't pay much attention that first time, as I was out rambling, but made a mental note to find out more about it and resolved to ask my father when I returned home.

Rambling is good for the soul as it brings us back to the time when we all were nomads, with no constraints, and in the soft, warm, misty Irish rain it is a wonderful, almost spiritual experience. There is a sense of freedom that's truly intoxicating. I went rambling most days after school and looked forward to the weekends. The secret was to get off the road as soon as possible and as I knew where all the openings in the hedges and the gaps in the walls were, I could be in that other wild, parallel world of nature in minutes.

The smell of wet heather wafts and mingles with the sweet aroma of the open countryside. The stillness seems to envelop all. I would pause and listen for the *caws* of the crows atop the branches of a sprawling oak tree or the melodic song of a goldfinch as he called his mate from a patch of thistles. Sometimes, a startled rabbit, scared by a wily fox, would dart out from beneath a tangle of gorse bushes, his large brown eyes wide with fear as he ran for safety. Off in the distance the faint lowing of grazing cows could be heard if I stopped and was perfectly still. Then the quiet would descend again, dropping slowly. Later that night I asked my father about the rock. He settled in his favorite armchair, rolled a cigarette from his tobacco tin and with smoke curling up toward the ceiling, in a hushed, almost reverent voice, he related the story.

The rock had been placed there soon after the Penal Law was enacted in Ireland in 1607. This law was imposed in retaliation for two major events that occurred earlier. The first was the failed *Gunpowder plot* of 1605 in which a group of English Catholics tried to blow up the *Houses of Parliament* in London. The second event took place in early 1607 when a group of Irish noblemen left for Europe to enlist Catholic aid for another revolt against the English crown. This became known as the *Flight of the Earls*. The Penal law was enacted by the newly crowned king of England and Ireland James I. James, the son of Mary Queen of Scots, was a noted and prolific author, widely known for compiling two important books; the King James version of the bible and a guide book on the subject of witchcraft and how to identify witches, titled *Daemonologie*. The pilgrims would bring copies of these writings with them to the new world and use them with terrifying results, in Salem, Mass.

The Penal law was strictly enforced by most notably, the Puritan Oliver Cromwell who invaded Ireland in 1649 with his new Model Army, and proceeded to subdue the population with a series of violent, repressive military campaigns. The hope was that within one generation, Catholicism would be eradicated. After the 1641 rebellion, Ireland was under the control of the Irish Confederate Catholics and an alliance was formed with the English Royalists led by the charismatic Charles II the son of Charles I, who had been executed for supposed treason. The law took away all rights from Catholics and effectively banished Bishops. Priests were required to register to preach after this date, but few obeyed this law, as it would require an oath of allegiance to the English crown, if they refused were deemed guilty of high treason and faced death, or at best, exile.

Always, an isolated location with a commanding view of the surrounding area would be chosen and a rock taken most times from a demolished Church would be placed there. It would have a simple cross carved on top, consecrated, and at that precise moment, become a Mass Rock. The faithful would huddle there in silence, usually at night, rain or shine, fearful and ever watchful for the appearance of the authorities. Their faith was all that sustained them. The dreaded *Priest Hunters* scoured the countryside hoping to collect the bounty placed on the head of every Priest. My father went on to explain that what all those people wanted to do was to gather there in honor of some man from a place called Galilee who had sacrificed himself for the greater good of mankind. I was convinced that Galilee was somewhere up the Creamery road, but I swear, in all the rambling I did, I never found it there. Lookouts would be posted to warn of any patrols approaching and when the all clear was given, the Priest would make his appearance and wearing a veil, say Mass. The faithful would respond in whispers and fear would be dominant. If he was ever caught performing this secret ritual, he was executed on the spot. The veil hopefully ensured that he could not be identified by anyone should they be questioned. Thankfully, the Penal Law was abolished in the latter part of the 1800's. Many of these Mass Rocks survive and still dot the Irish landscape today. They serve as a constant reminder of those dark and frightening times and attest to the indomitable and undaunted, Irish spirit.

The Rowan Tree

Another Lesson on History

I could see for miles from my vantage point in the topmost branches of the Rowan tree that grew next to our house in Urker. It was my favorite of all the trees in the area with the big Oak next. In the summer, with the leaves in full profusion, I could stay hidden forever if I chose to. When my sisters were outside I would sometimes throw small twigs at them. I admit that I laughed silently when they couldn't see where the missiles were coming from. It was a great tree and a perfect hiding place. More than a hundred years old, all around the trunk were lots of carvings and heart shapes. I carved my initials one day with an old pocket knife my father had given me once when we were out fishing. I loved to climb, especially when I knew there was a bird's nest hidden somewhere in the branches. My father told us a story about the Rowan tree one night as we sat around the fire. It was the winter time and snow covered everything in a pure, glistening white blanket. The wind howled outside but we were warmed by the blazing log fire in the open hearth. My mother had baked soda bread earlier that afternoon and as we sat with our cups of steaming cocoa and slices of the still warm bread smothered in melting butter, my father settled back in his armchair and began to tell the story.

"There are several trees growing in Ireland that the Druids believed had very special powers. They believed that each one had its own specific place in the order of things and had medicinal qualities, which could cure many ailments. The Rowan tree was the most important one and the Druids revered it."

" Who were the Druids?" I asked, puzzled.

"They were the sages and seers that guided the Celts, our ancestors," he answered.

"What are sages and seers," I enquired again.

"They were wise men and were very, very powerful." He explained that the Druids were a priestly sect who accompanied the Celts as they migrated across Europe.

"Was there someone chasing them?"

"Yes. The Roman army was after them and wished to stamp them out."

" Why Didn't the Romans like them?"

" It wasn't a matter of liking them; it was about fearing them. Now, let's get on with the story."

I looked over at my mother who was sitting in her chair knitting, and saw her smiling. She was listening to the story too. My sisters were playing with her cat in the hallway but I don't think they were listening. My father stretched toward the log box, picked out a fat log and placed in on the now dwindling embers. As he did, a rush of brightly colored sparks exploded and rushed up the chimney, carried aloft by the thick plumes of smoke. The cat, which had just sauntered in the room at that moment froze in her tracks and with a loud frightened *meow* jumped on my mothers' lap for comfort and safety. When all of this commotion died down my father continued the story.

"The Rowan tree is also known as the *traveler's tree*, and anyone going on a journey would always carry a sprig to protect them and ensure that they would arrive safely." "Like a lucky penny?" "Yes, but more powerful than a lucky penny." "The Druid always carried a long staff which he would cut from a Rowan tree as he believed it had magical powers." "Like a magic wand!" I asked excitedly. I was listening intently by this time. "Not quite, a magic wand is short a staff is a lot longer."

"In fact," he added, almost as if he had just remembered it, "Saint Patrick, when he returned to Ireland as a newly appointed Bishop, went to the nearest Rowan tree and cut his first staff from it."

I was still confused over the difference between a wand and a staff. "A dowsing rod would also be cut from the Rowan tree," continued my father. Now I was completely baffled. "Dowsing rod?" I queried, lost. "Who. St. Patrick?" I was trying to visualize St. Patrick climbing a Rowan tree and wondered aloud, "Was St. Patrick a Druid?" "What are you talking about?" Now my father appeared as puzzled as I was. "You said he cut his dowsing rod from the Rowan tree," I answered, totally bewildered. My mother was laughing loudly now and I could hear my sisters sniggering in the hallway. They were always sniggering! So they *were* listening after all! "No, not St. Patrick. I meant that the *Druid* cut his dowsing rod from the tree. Saint Patrick cut his staff from it."

" Oh. I see," I said, embarrassed. My sisters were giggling like silly idiots by then and when my father wasn't looking, I stuck my tongue out and glared at them and resolved to throw lots of twigs at them the next time I climbed the tree. Even the silly cat seemed to be grinning. "Now, where was I?" "The dowsing rod, Mal," hinted my mother. "What's a dowsing rod? I queried again, still puzzled.

"The Druid used a dowsing rod for many purposes. For example, if he wanted to find the perfect place to set up a new village he would dowse the area until he found the *ley* lines. Or to find the place to use as a sacred spot for worship, it's also used to find water underground," he explained. I again glanced over at my mother looking for clues but she was intent on her knitting "What are *ley lines?*" "*Ley lines* are underground energy sources." He got up, went into the hallway and returned holding a slender branch that looked like a large letter Y. Holding the Y shaped branch aloft he announced, "This, is a dowsing rod." Then holding a leg of the branch in each hand and pointing the other end straight ahead, he walked back and forth across the floor. "When water is detected, the rod will move and point downward showing you where the source is. So you see, the Rowan tree is very special." " And," he quipped, "a *good* magician always cut his wand from a Rowan tree." My mother got up then, put the knitting in her basket, set the cat on the floor, smoothed her dress, and said, "Bedtime girls and boys, school in the morning."

The Clock

A Lesson on Patience

Like most inquisitive men, my father Mal had a penchant for dismantling and re-assembling various objects, he felt sure needed improvement. It did not matter what the object was or how big. He believed that he could improve any object by simply applying his innate genius and therefore make it much better than it was before. One night he decided to put his clock making skills to good use. "Your ancestors were skilled in the art of metalworking and were well known and admired all over the civilized world." He was of course, referring to the Celts. He was always bragging about them. He depended on an old, wind-up alarm clock to rouse him in the mornings but was certain that it ticked much slower than it should. That evening, I was sitting on the floor in the living room with my sisters trying to piece together a jigsaw puzzle. My mother was in the kitchen baking pies, her cat at her feet, the aroma wafting from the kitchen spread throughout the house and made us all hungry. My father was sitting in his favorite red armchair and I noticed he was drumming his fingers on the armrest. That meant he was deep in thought. I knew something was afoot. As we sorted through the pieces of the puzzle, I saw him rise from the chair and go to his bedroom.

After a few minutes, he returned clutching the old wind up clock. He sat back in his chair and held the clock up close as if he was inspecting it. He shook it once or twice and held it to his ear. Then, he wound it and shook it again. "Too slow," he grumbled as he placed it on the table beside his chair and stared at it. He called me over to his side and with a finger to his lips said, "Shhh, listen, do you hear that?" and pointed at the clock. I bent down close to the clock and could clearly hear the *tick tock, tick tocking* sound. "Yes, I can hear it dad." "Well, what do you think?"
The clock sounded fine to me, but what did I know at seven years of age. "It's much too slow. It should be ticking much faster than that," he said impatiently. I knew what was coming next and ran to get his small toolbox from the bottom shelf of the dresser. Thus, it was that he determined to improve the slowly ticking clock. "Are you sure about this, Mal?" my mother inquired innocently as she stepped in from the kitchen, her hands and apron covered in flour.
"Ellen, anybody with an ounce of common sense could do this," he said with a snort of derision.
"It's in the genes, woman."
He then went on to remind that the Celts could do anything with metal; they were past masters.
"In fact," he added, "They traded their wares with the Romans!"

What all this Roman business had to do with clocks, I didn't know. He then cleared the table, spread the newspaper, produced one small screwdriver from the toolbox and with the precision of a brain surgeon, proceeded to take the clock apart. Several hours later, the table was a maze of springs, cog wheels, nuts and bolts, and whatever else a clock may include. After carefully inspecting, oiling, and cleaning each individual part, he started the re-assembly process. With the patience that only a madman or a man locked up for life has, my father, the clockmaker, methodically and painstakingly started to put the clock back together.

By that time, it was getting very late and with eyes drooping, I crawled off into bed and slept. I woke early the next morning, and with thoughts of the dismantled clock still fresh in my mind, ran to the kitchen, where, there on the table was the fully assembled clock, ticking away loudly. I was truly amazed.

My father had sat up all night and completed his mission. On closer inspection, I saw, on the table, beside the clock, two small springs, and one small, shiny cog wheel. My father swore from that day forward, that those extra parts were the cause of the problem all along. I swear, to this day, whenever I hear *Time* by Pink Floyd and those ringing and ticking clocks at the beginning of the track, I smile, and I am certain that Mal smiles too, up there with his *people*.

The Fly

A Lesson on Determination

We were all at home that night. My mother, seated in her comfortable armchair reading a book, the cat curled at her feet, purring contentedly. My two younger sisters played quietly with their dolls. I idly turned the pages of an often read comic book and cast regular glances at my father. I sensed he was planning something. I could always tell. At seven, I was curious about everything, especially when my father was about to start a project. I could always read the tell-tale signs whenever he had an idea in mind. That night as he sat in his chair, an open newspaper in his lap he drummed his fingers on the armrest. That was a *sure* sign. The gentle *hiss* of the oil lamp was a comforting sound and the *crackle* from the logs burning brightly in the hearth made for a cozy, warm feeling of security.

Suddenly, he folded the newspaper, placed it on the table beside his chair, and picked up his tobacco tin. I watched as he opened it and removed a small rectangular piece of paper. He took some tobacco and spread it on the paper, then, using both hands, deftly rolled a cigarette. He licked the exposed edge of the paper, completed the roll, and carefully removed the excess tobacco from both ends. This he always placed back in the tin. Then, with a flourish like a magician, he would hold the finished product up in the air as if it were a trophy "Perfect!" he would exclaim and displaying his hands to us, ask,

"Who am I going to leave these hands to when I am gone?"

At this we all laughed, even though we had heard him say it many times before. He lit the cigarette and sat back enjoying the aroma and taste of his latest creation. I knew he was now deep in thought but also knew that my impatience would have to be controlled until the exact moment. As the cigarette smoke curled slowly upward toward the ceiling I glanced at the cat and watched as she arched her back, stretch lazily and with a wide yawn settle back down at my mother's feet. It was then that my father spoke.

"*Now!*" I thought.

"I was talking to a man today about fishing," he said.

"Who were you talking to Mal," enquired my mother as she turned a page.

"James from up the road, and he used *that* word again."

"*Impossible?*" she queried.

"Yes, it seems to be his favorite word."

"What did he say was impossible on this occasion?"

"Oh. I told him I could catch a rainbow trout with a home-made fly and he laughed at me and said it was impossible."

"Can you do that?"

"I don't know, but I know that nothing is impossible, it can't be that difficult." He finished his cigarette, stood up and emptied the ashtray in the fireplace, as he turned he said to me,

"I'm going to show you a trick, bring me a piece of paper and a pencil."

I ran to my school bag and took out my blue writing book and pencil and laid them on the table. My father took the pencil and wrote the word IMPOSSIBLE in large letters across a blank page.

"Whenever you see or hear this word it means that something cannot be done. Now watch what happens when I do this."

He took the pencil, drew a vertical line between the M and the P, and wrote it once more in its new form. It now appeared like this: IM POSSIBLE. He had made two new words. I silently mouthed the words I'm Possible, several times and repeated them out loud which made my father laugh. "Good boy! Think of this every time anyone tells you that you *can't* do something, that it's *impossible*"

"I will remember it I promise."

I could no longer contain my excitement, as now I *knew* what was coming next. He was going to make a fly! I jumped up, knocking the chair to the floor and raced over to the dresser where inside on the bottom shelf he kept a small square tool-box. I picked it up and ran back to the table where he was already spreading the newspaper. He opened the box and took from it a small vise, a pair of pliers, a little green bottle, and a magnifying glass. From a coat pocket he removed several colored feathers and a roll of very fine thread. Then from another he took a bottle cork and laid everything neatly on the table. He reached up to where the oil lamp hung from the ceiling and pumped the handle several times. When he did this, the *hiss* got louder and the light got brighter.

"That's better," he said. "Now we can see everything clearly."

"Always check that you have enough light and all the parts before you start," he advised.

"Do we have all the parts?"

He lifted the cork from the table and I noticed it had something shiny attached. "We do now," he said as he removed a fish hook from the cork and held it out for me to see.

"Always use a cork when you handle fish hooks, it's safer that way."

"I will."

I picked up a small, yellow feather off the table and held it up to the light. It was so fine I could see through it and I remember thinking how delicate it was and how vivid and bright the color.

"It's perfect," I said.

"That one belonged to a goldfinch," explained my father.

"And this one," he said as he pointed to a glossy, dark blue, almost black one, "once belonged to a blackbird."

"Who owned this? I asked as I gingerly held out a scarlet colored one.

"That one," he said, peering at it closely, "belonged to a red robin."

"Will they still be able to fly?"

"Oh yes!" he laughed, "Birds have lots of feathers. They grow new ones every year."

At ease now, I settled back in the chair and watched as he placed the hook in the vise and closed the jaws. He then stripped several strands from each feather and set them aside. Using his magnifying glass, he placed red strands on either side of the hook and wound the thread around tightly.

Then he overlaid the dark ones and tied them in the same way. He repeated this with the yellow feathers and suddenly the hook was transformed.

"We're not finished yet," he said. "We have to glue the threads and make them waterproof."

"Why do they have to be waterproof?"

"So they won't come apart when we get them wet."

With delicate snips, he trimmed the feathers using a pair of my mother's scissors and dabbed adhesive from the small bottle, along the spine of the hook. He held it up and gently blew on it a few times, then, handed it to me saying, "Don't forget the cork!"

I stuck the sharp end of the hook into the cork and held it up to the light peering at it through the magnifying glass. The bare fishing hook had become a beautiful, brightly colored fly!

"Tomorrow we will go and introduce our fly to Mr. Trout," announced my father. And early the next morning, we did.

The Trout

A Lesson on Defeating Naysayers

"Do you remember the trick I showed you last night?" asked my father as we crossed the low, stone wall that separated us from the river.

"Nothing is impossible!" I burst out, remembering.

"Good boy, you remembered. Nothing is impossible," he repeated as we walked along the bank of the river searching for the ideal spot. It was a perfect morning with the sun not yet too hot. The green pasture rolled out before us sloping gently on its' way to the river's edge. A small flock of grazing sheep silently ate the lush grass, not even stopping to look up as we passed by.

The strong scent of the gorse bushes that ran down from the wall all the way to the riverbank, was heady. A large hare, roused by the sound of our voices revealed her hiding place and with a startled leap, sprinted off into the distance.

We were going to try and lure a rainbow trout using for the first time, a fly that my father had created the night before. I with a fishing rod he had fashioned using a long piece of bamboo and he with a fly-fishing rod that he had assembled from several old cast offs. I peeked inside the metal can to check on the mass of worms and grubs that I had dug up earlier that morning from our garden and shrugged my shoulder to position my bag more securely. "This looks like a good spot," he announced as he dropped his fishing bag on the ground. All around the river bank, grew a thick profusion of water reeds and on the opposite bank stood a majestic white oak tree in full leaf, its arms spread wide, invitingly. Several glossy, black crows nested in the higher branches, their *caws* falling silent when they realized that we were going to stay for a while. Next to the oak grew a leafy hazel tree. Further, down the riverbank, several frogs croaked rhythmically as they hopped from lily pad to lily pad. As we assembled our rods, the crows eyed us suspiciously.

I watched as my father took a reel out of his fishing bag, walk across the field to a nearby gorse bush, and tie the end of the line to a small branch. Then, holding the spinning reel in both hands he walked back towards me, the line stretching out behind him. Handing me the reel he said, "Here, hold this."
From his pocket, he took a little round tin and removed the lid, then took a small white cloth from inside.
"What's that," I asked, pointing to the cream colored contents.
"This is wax for the line."

He smeared the cloth with wax and walking back towards the gorse bush coated the line with the wax, stopping to dip the cloth several times. Untying the line he turned and said, "Now, pretend that I'm a fish and reel me in."

As I reeled, he walked towards me stopping sometimes, making it difficult for me to turn the reel. Then laughing, he would walk a little bit closer, stop, walk again until finally, the line was ready. "Why do you wax the line?"

"So that it will float on the water and not sink."

"Always try to fish close to a hazel tree," he advised.

"Why a hazel tree?"

"Because if you catch a trout or a salmon under a hazel, chances are they will have eaten some of the ripe nuts that drop in the water."

As I struggled with the wriggling worm, I was unsuccessfully trying to coax onto the hook I asked,

"Why, are hazel nuts good?"

"They are the best and the fish love them. The ones that have eaten them are fatter and tastier"

He further explained that in ancient Ireland the Celts worshipped the hazel tree and believed that it possessed special power. Anyone who eats a fish that has eaten its berries, gains that same power.

"Who were the Celts?"

"They were the people who lived in Ireland a long, long time ago."

"Are they still living here now?

"Oh yes," he said, "they live on through us and are our ancestors."

"I see," I said, puzzled, not seeing at all.

"Will you tell me about them?"

"Of course I will, but not now. Now we have to catch Mr. Trout."

"You promise?"

"I promise," he said and with that, he waded into the shallows and started casting. *Swissssh* went the line as he cast the fly toward a spot further up the river from the oak tree. We watched as the fly floated on the surface and drift with the current. He let it float past the oak and then pulled the rod back sharply and cast again. *Swissssh.* I tried once more to get the worm to cooperate and silently begged it to get on my hook. A loud *Splash* suddenly grabbed my attention and startled me so much I dropped the worm and the fishing rod. The frightened crows took flight from the tree and with angry *caws*, took off for somewhere quieter.

"I've got one!" exclaimed my father jubilantly, "Get the net!" He had indeed hooked a large trout. As it fought the line, it leaped high out of the water, twisting and turning trying to dislodge the hook from its jaw.

Another loud *Splash* occurred as it descended and hit the water, and I watched in amazement as, my father began reeling it in. Again, it leaped, this time even higher and I could see the myriad of green, blue, and gold speckled dots on its body and understood then why it was called a *rainbow* trout. I was mesmerized and the excitement was almost overpowering. *Splash* again, it hit the water and as it did, I noticed my father let go of the reel lock.

"Don't let him go dad," I shouted, tripping over the bag and falling on the grass. "Always let him run a little," he said.

Puzzled, I asked, "Why do you let him run?"

"So he will get tired."

"Won't he get away?"

"No, once he's hooked he won't get away."

I watched as the line tightened and darted off, first in one direction then suddenly turned sharply and shot off in the opposite direction. "He's a fighter," laughed my father and as I looked at him, I could see beads of perspiration running down his face, his eyes bright and wide with concentration.

"Bring the net over here," he said as his hat fell off.

He pointed with his foot to a spot on the river bank.

"Here," he motioned. "Get ready!"

As I stood there with the net, the trout gave another huge leap, high in the air, wriggling furiously and then with a final *Splash* hit the surface of the water, sending ripples all the way to the opposite bank. "Now we've got him!" he exclaimed, breathless. I stared with nervous excitement as my father reeled the trout in slowly, pausing occasionally to let him run, then reel in again. *Reel and pause. Reel and pause.* I could now clearly see the fish as he neared the river bank, tired and about to give up but still fighting.

"Slide the net under him slowly."

"Like this?"

"Yes, just like that."

I watched in wonder as my father skillfully and with great patience guided the trout into the net. In one swift, fluid move he dropped his fishing rod, grabbed the handle of the net and together we landed the large fish "Good boy; well done. Best bit of fishing I've ever seen!" he exuded.

He took a small pair of pliers out of his bag and removed the fly from the fish's mouth. Then he picked up his fallen hat, slapped it against his thigh, and stuck the hook in the hat band for safety. It was a big fat trout but as I picked up the fishing bag, I felt a twinge of pity for it, as it lay there helpless on the grass. My father sensing my discomfort said gently, "Don't feel sorry for him, fish are created for us to eat, that is the role they are meant to play."

"I know but I can't help it dad."

"Don't worry, you will get over it, I promise."

With that, he put his arm around my shoulder, picked my rod off the ground, handed it to me, and said with a wink and a grin,

"Now, it's your turn."

By sundown on that magical day, we had caught four fat Trout and I carried them proudly in my fishing bag. When we arrived home, I ran into the kitchen to show them to my mother. My father picked out the fattest one and wrapped it in newspaper. He then handed it to me and said,

"Take this up to James, and tell him I sent you."

The Garden

A Lesson on Hard Work

The last battle fought in Ireland between two kings took place on July 12. 1690. It happened on the banks of the river Boyne, near the town of Drogheda. The catholic king James was defeated by the protestant king William, of the Belgian house of Orange. Ever since then, the protestant population, fondly called Orangemen, burn large bonfires, and anything catholic, in celebration of that glorious event every July 12th.

To the left of our house in Urker, was a wilderness covered with boulders, and thorny gorse bushes. It was no more than a quarter acre, but to me, at seven years old it looked like a vast, forbidding jungle. It was around that time that my father was stricken with a severe bout of insanity. He decided one night, to become a farmer. "Anyone with an ounce of common sense could do that," he snorted. In 1950, he brought my mother and me to Crossmaglen for the first time and rented a cottage in Annamar, a small farming community, about two miles outside the town. There he would have observed his neighbors tilling and sowing their land with the greatest of ease. I believe that was where he got his inspiration and I hold those neighbors solely responsible for the nightmare I went through that spring and summer of 1956. I was duly recruited and drilled into becoming a not so merry ploughboy. Armed with a pick, shovel, and an old spade that he borrowed from a friend, we both at that moment became farmers and began to till the soil. "It's all about drainage, drainage is the key."

He took his coat off and hung it on a branch of the Holly tree that stood by the side of the house, then, after taking a long drink of water, handed me the bottle. He walked all around the garden then taking long, slow strides, stopping every now and then to look back toward the stream. I followed in his footsteps and had to run to keep up with him, sometimes tripping and falling over a twisted root or a jutting rock.

"What are we doing this for?"

"We're taking the measurements. We need to know where to put the drains." Occasionally, neighbors would stop by to observe the goings on and to offer tidbits of wisdom. I recall one in particular who stood and watched for a half hour as we toiled, then after tapping his pipe on the heel of his boot, offered an opinion to my father.

"Mal, you must be mad. You're wasting your time nothing will grow there. There are too many rocks. If I was you I wouldn't bother with all that digging and hard work. You would be better off if you bought your vegetables from the grocer as I do. Save yourself a lot of sweat, not to mention the blisters."

"Ahh… is that yourself James?" said my father, then in a low voice muttered under his breath, "Fukkin' gobshite."

My father had also perfected the age old art of muttering, meaning he could say things under his breath that could only be heard if you were standing very close to him. "Well James, time will tell and anyway, it keeps me out of the pub." James, who visited the local pub every day, visibly reddened and shuffled from one foot to the other. It was well known that his wife was not pleased with James' daily excursions and could often be heard berating him loudly. As his composure recovered, James went on to give numerous other reasons as to why it was impossible to do what we were attempting. My father let him have his say and when he had finished, he said simply,

"As I said James, time will tell."

With that, James turned on his heel and walked, unsteadily, off up the road. We watched him for a while, then resumed our labors.

"That was one of the naysayers. You will meet plenty of them in your lifetime. Always let them have their say, then redouble your efforts."

He hated naysayers with a passion and explained that they will give you a hundred reasons as to why something can't be done, but never one positive reason as to how it could. This encounter only spurred my father on. Talk about slash and burn! It was as if he was possessed. He laid into the gorse bushes like a Crusader re-taking Jerusalem, and by the end of that first day, we had a bonfire ten feet high that any *Orangeman* worth his salt would have paid good British pounds for, on the eve of the twelfth of July. I often thought years later that selling gorse bushes to *Orangemen,* as fuel for their bonfires would be a great way to earn a few pounds. It might be better than scouring the streets for empties, as I did later on. When the heat from the bonfire died down, we started on the boulders and rocks and soon we had a stack of rocks and stones that any Norman invader bent on castle building, would have died for. It was then that I first heard him utter the dreaded word, *trenching.*

Trenching is the ancient art of draining any area prone to holding water because of poor soil quality. This is where the pick and shovel were utilized and dad and I set about digging the first trench. "Pick," he ordered and as I was in the role of quartermaster that day, I handed him the pick. He rolled up his sleeves, spat on his hands and with a *stand back boy,* command, commenced to assault the earth with a fervor equaled only in later years, when groups of hardy souls dug their way out of many British prison camps.

He started at the far end of the garden, for that's how he now envisioned it, and dug a trench two feet wide and a foot and a half deep all the way to the stream that ran along the roadside, a distance of one hundred feet or so. Over the course of the next two weeks, we dug two more identical trenches. It was at that moment in time I was given my first glimpse of the connection with the ancients.

"I'm going to show you how your ancestors did this. We need two types of flat stones." He then proceeded to instruct me in how to select from the rock pile the two types. The narrow ones were the *standing stones* and the wider ones would be the *cap stones.* After a week of sorting and shifting, we had our beginning inventory. We then lined the sides of each trench with the narrower *standing stones,* filled the bottoms with gravel and smaller stones to a depth of a foot or so, and then laid the wider *cap stones* on top, creating a tunnel effect. The whole area we topped off with a mixture of sharp sand, peat from the bog a distance behind the house, cow dung donated by a neighbor from his farmyard and a load of horse manure and straw donated by another neighbor, a celebrated horse breeder. The land was now ready for planting.   It was only years later that I realized he had built his trenches using the exact same construction principles the ancients used in building their megaliths. How did he know? It must be in the genes! In fact, what we had created were miniature replicas of the *passage graves and court cairns*, that still dot the landscape all over Ireland. Beginning that summer and right up until the day we left Urker, each year we had bumper crops of potatoes, carrots, parsnips, onions, turnips, peas, leeks, scallions and every herb known to man. Along one side of the garden were numerous gooseberry and blackcurrant bushes. On the opposite side, we had a forest of rhubarb plants. On another side, he planted a variety of flowers and shrubs that would put any botanical garden to shame. Coupled with the eggs my mother's hens laid daily, and the trout and salmon my father caught in the local river, we were a poor but well fed and very happy family. He called me one evening, later that first summer, to the garden.

"Bring these up to James's house," he said, as he handed me a large box of assorted vegetables, fruits and a bunch of mixed flowers.

"Tell him I sent you."

Then, almost as an aside, he said to me with a wink,

"This is how you handle the naysayers."

Bringing Home The Bacon

A Lesson on Sustenance

Sigmund Freud, the noted psychoanalyst once commented, exasperated, "Psychiatry is wasted on the Irish." How true this is I cannot say, but had Sigmund ever met my father, he would have had a field day and may even have learned something. Mal was mad; there was no doubt about that. Ask anyone. So much so some of the local children who were budding geniuses, behind his back, dubbed him *Mad Mal*. They never to my knowledge said it within earshot and certainly not to his face. They knew better! Although not a physical man, he was wiry and there was a distinct aura around him. He often told me that it is the inner strength that moves the mountain. I am sure that you have heard it said that a man must bring home the bacon. My father did just that, literally and I was there when that unforgettable event took place. We were living in a rented, two storied house about a mile outside the town. As the upper floor area was not livable, due to the floorboards either rotted or missing, we lived on the ground floor. It was a fairly large house and we were comfortable there.

I lived there from age two to age ten with my mother Ellen, my father Mal, and my younger sisters, Teresa and Marion, and of course, Magilligan! He was the bacon that my father brought home, kicking, and squealing. My father had already had him baptized and christened. Indeed, it happened on the way down the road from my Uncle Joe's house. Where he came up with the name we never did find out, but I suspect that it had something to do with the barman of one local hostelry in the town who was famous for brewing a mixture of lemonade and beer fondly called *shandy*. Mal was known to imbibe, on a warm day, a glass, or two of that sweet elixir, purely for slaking the thirst of course! He arrived home one afternoon and called to us, "Come on out and meet Magilligan." We scrambled out into the front garden and watched as my father unbuttoned his long brown coat. Something wriggled underneath and let out several loud squeals as my father bent down and released a small, pink piglet, which immediately took off running. We ran around the garden trying to catch him and I am sure that we squealed louder than the little runt. My father stood by the front wall and roared with laughter. Suddenly the piglet made a sharp left turn and bolted in through the open front door. We stopped dead in our tracks, not knowing what to do next. The squealing stopped and we all fell silent looking at each other. Just then, my mother appeared in the doorway and in her arms was the piglet, quiet as a mouse. My mother, being a practical woman was more concerned with bacon that you put on a frying pan with some fresh eggs, not the four legged variety, enquired in her unique cool, calm kind of way, "When will he be ready to eat, Mal?"

I saw my father quickly put his finger to his lips and say "*Shhh,*" to my mother. She walked over to me and handed me the piglet. He looked up at me and I swear, as I peered at his pink snout and his little piggy eyes, I saw him smile! From that moment, we became best friends. He followed me everywhere and with excited *oinks* and *squeals,* we roamed the fields behind the house together every day after school. He quickly developed the habit of bathing in the mornings soon after he discovered the stream that ran between our vegetable garden and the road. At first, he was wary of the water but seeing me splash and slosh he decided it was time to get his feet wet. Soon he was wallowing and squealing with delight. This became a daily ritual that we both enjoyed immensely. I felt sorry for my mother's ducks and chickens when Magilligan decided to chase them around the yard. Her cat would freeze when she heard the first *oink* and run immediately for cover.

If you stood on the creamery road facing the house you would have seen, a small shed with a flat thatched roof on the right. This became his home, provided you could entice him to enter. For a runt, he sure could run and I swear he kept us all on our toes! You must understand the psychology behind this whole pig business. My father had a plan. Purchase a pig, fatten him up and when the time is right, you've guessed it, *bacon!* The catchword around our house became *save your scraps.* He was fed like a king and there were times when I believed his dinner looked more appetizing than mine did. I took part in his fattening process wholeheartedly and discovered that he had a fondness for chocolate. Every morning, I led him across the road to our neighbor Mr. Smith's gates.

There, everyday like clockwork, the milkman deposited four bottles of milk, two regular and two extra creamy. I would carefully remove the bottle tops, pour the milk on the ground and watch with delight as Magilligan lapped it up with relish. I did leave one bottle of each untouched, for Mr. Smith though. When the milk was finished he would lick his chops, and after an expectant glance at the remaining bottles, trot off for his morning forage. One morning as we arrived at the gates I noticed something very odd. There was no milk! *Magilligan* saw it too and looked at me in bewilderment. Then, with a contemptuous snort, he wandered off in the direction of our house, his tail curled tightly. It was later that I found out Mr. Smith had instructed the milkman to leave the milk inside the gates in the future.

The time went on and Magilligan got bigger, so big I often sat on his back and rode around the garden pretending to be a cowboy with guns blazing, shooting at my mother's chickens and ducks. If the cat should venture out, we would chase her too. In the mornings when I left for school, he would follow me along the creamery road until we arrived at the main road and there we would part. As I walked towards the town, I would look back over my shoulder and sure enough, he would still be there. He headed for home only when I had disappeared over the brow of the hill. I can still remember my anticipation each day as I reached the hill on my way home and looked down in the distance to the Creamery road and there he would be, waiting patiently. He would run to meet me and knew that I would have a bar of chocolate for him to feast on. I loved that pig and I believe the feeling was mutual.

Eventually, the dreaded day came when Magilligan the martyr had to accept his destiny, as had I, and offer himself up on the altar of sustenance. I was told later by Mal the butcher that he went to meet his fate with the dignity of a Celtic warrior. I was heartbroken and missed him terribly. From that day to this, anytime I smell the sweet aroma of sizzling bacon, the memories come flooding back, and I stop, look upwards and with a smile and a wink, offer a silent thanks to Magilligan.

Teddy

A Lesson on Adoption

Our house was quiet after Magilligan left us and I missed him terribly and was angry with my father for a long time. We still had the cat and my mother's ducks and chickens but they were not the same. Every day I hoped and prayed that he would somehow come back and we could have fun together again. Walking to school became a sad ritual and coming home was even worse. One Sunday about two weeks later, my father came home from the early mass and called me out into the front yard. As I stepped outside my father was leaning his bicycle against the wall.

"Come here, I have something to show you." I was still angry with him and he must have seen the dour look on my face because he said,

"I'm sorry about Magilligan and I know that you loved him, that's why I brought you this." With that, he opened his coat and brought out a little black and white dog. "Here, this is for you."

I took the dog in my arms and laughed when it licked my face.

"What's his name?"

"I don't know, we will have to choose a name for him."

"Thanks dad," I called over my shoulder as I ran inside to show my mother and sisters.

Later that afternoon I overheard my father telling my mother how he found the dog. As he was leaving our local church, Saint Patrick's, where he sang in the choir, he noticed a small black and white dog sitting at the bottom of the church steps. The dog seemed lost and didn't look healthy at all, in fact, he seemed half starved. My father waited until the mass crowd had dispersed and noticed that the dog was still there. Without further ado, Mal, the one man adoption agency, picked him up, put him under his coat, and transported him by bicycle, to his new home. You, I am sure, can imagine the excitement when this new addition to our family arrived. A list of names was compiled and the name Teddy was chosen, by my youngest sister Marion. Teddy became, from that moment, my rambling companion. I was born a rambler and nothing pleased me more than disappearing over the fields and into that other world of nature and serenity. When you have a companion, it is so much better.

My new rambling companion was the black and white collie named Teddy. I taught him how to sit and how to fetch sticks. We roamed the fields every day after school chasing rabbits and he could sure run fast. Teddy filled the void left by Magilligan and we spent many happy days together.

The Goldfinch

A Lesson on Ingenuity

One day I watched my father from high up in the branches of the old Rowan tree that grew close to our house. He was walking down the creamery road, his brown felt hat pushed back on his head and I could hear him whistling. As he neared our house, I saw that he was swinging something big in his left hand. I clambered down the tree, swung from the lowest branch, dropped to the ground and ran to meet him.

"Dad, what's that?"

"This," he said as he held it aloft, "is a cage for a Goldfinch."

"What's a Goldfinch?"

"It's a very small, beautiful songbird," he replied.

"But we don't have any birds," I reminded him.

"No we don't," he smiled and added, but we will tomorrow.

"Tonight we must prepare his new home."

That meant a project!

He handed me the cage and walked over to the tree, reached up and selected three small, thin branches and snapped them off. Then he carefully removed the leaves and said "These will be perfect, just what we need!"

He removed a bunch of Mistletoe that was growing around a large branch and put it in his pocket.

I ran inside and got the toolbox from the bottom shelf of the dresser and set in on the floor beside the table in readiness. He spread some newspaper and placed the birdcage on the table. The cage looked perfect to me but my father said,

"See, there are no perches."

"What are perches for?"

"They are where he will sit, look, I'll show you."

He picked up one length of Rowan twig and measured the space between the bars of the cage. Then he marked the length on the rod with a pencil. With his small saw, he cut it to size and made a notch on either end then slid the rod through the bars. He did the same thing with two more rods. "Now Mr. Goldfinch can sit wherever he wishes," he laughed.

Next, he attached two small square containers, one on each side of the cage, close to a perch.

"These are for his seed and water."

The third perch he placed higher up in the cage, about half way.

He took the mistletoe from his pocket then and started to mash it until it became a sticky liquid. As he poured it into a small glass jar, I asked him what it he was doing. "You will see tomorrow," was his reply.

I hardly slept at all that night thinking about the birdcage and wondered what a Goldfinch might look like.

I was up early the next morning and found my father sitting at the kitchen table. He was sipping tea from his large mug and had a pile of buttered toast in front of him.

"Do you want some tea?"

"Yes, I do," I answered, yawning.

As I ate, he poured tea in my mother's favorite cup and brought it into the bedroom.

"Are we going for Mr. Goldfinch now"? I asked, impatiently.

"Yes we are, as soon as you finish your breakfast."

While I was finishing the last slice of toast, I noticed my father put two silver bottle caps in his pocket. I thought that it was a strange thing to do, but said nothing. I grabbed my coat from the rack in the hall and ran outside to wait for him. My father had a small shoe box under his arm as he stepped outside. He handed it to me saying,

"Don't drop it!"

As I looked, I noticed it had lots of holes.

"Those are air holes, so he can breathe.

"I won't drop it dad," I answered, holding it tightly.

"When we get to the right place we must be very quiet and still, birds are easily scared." It was a mild morning in July and as we walked along the road, I looked forward to the adventure. Crossing the low stone bridge that spanned the small gurgling stream, I heard something rustling in the hedgerow. My father heard it too and motioned me to stop. We stood perfectly still for several minutes and watched as a small, crafty looking, bright red Fox poked his head out of the bushes. Sniffing the air, he emerged stealthily, then, trotted across the road with his bushy tail following behind. A pair of startled blackbirds took flight from a whitethorn tree and flew off noisily in the opposite direction. The fox stopped and looked sadly after the retreating birds as if thinking, "There goes breakfast." Then, unhurried, he sauntered off to seek elsewhere. We walked on then and as we came near to the Mass rock my father stopped and said, "This is the place, we will go in here."

We were in front of a long stone wall that separated us from the fields. With one quick swing, he placed me on top of the wall, climbed up next to me and dropped effortlessly on the other side. Another swing and I was instantly transported to that other magical world of nature with no humans in sight, except for my father and me. We walked across the grassy meadow and came to a small rocky outcrop near an apple orchard. On one side was a shallow pond where several Eider ducks *quacked* fussily, their chicks in tow. On the opposite side there grew a thicket of small trees and bushes, all in full leaf. Between the pond and the thicket there was a large group of purple colored, thorny flowers growing in wild profusion. I had never seen that type of plant before and asked my father what they were.

"Those are Thistles," he answered.

Then added "Goldfinches love the seeds of the Thistles."

"Is this the place?"

"Yes, this is the place."

He walked over to a large rock beside the trees and with his back to it, sat down. "Bring me the box," he said as he motioned me to come over and sit beside him. I handed him the box and slid down the rock and sat on the cool grass. He opened the box and took from it the small glass jar. He reached in his pocket and brought out a little brush. After putting the lid back on the box, he set the jar and the brush on top of it. Next from the inside pocket of his jacket he took out the two silver bottle caps.

"I'm going to make a whistle for Mr. Goldfinch."

With that, he proceeded to bend and shape the bottle caps. He went about twining them together, then, putting his creation to his lips, he blew on it softly. The sound it made reminded me of a bird whistling. After some fine tuning, he handed it to me saying,

"Now, you try."

He showed me how to hold it and where to place my tongue just right. When I blew on it, it really sounded like a bird. He got up, went over to a small tree which was closest to the thistle flowers and removed the leaves from several small branches. With the brush, he smeared the adhesive on them then came back behind the rock and sat down. He put the bottle caps to his lips and started mimicking bird calls. As he was doing this, he pointed to the thistle patch and whispered,

"Watch closely."

I couldn't contain my excitement when, a few minutes later, three colorful birds lit on the thistle plants. They were twittering loudly answering my father's calls. He then tapped me on the shoulder and pointed to the small tree and whispered,

"Look!"

He stopped calling then and I held my breath as two more landed on the sticky branches. My father was up in a flash and running to the tree.

"Bring the box," he said excitedly.

When I reached the tree, he had already snapped the branches holding the two birds and handed one to me saying,

"Cover him with your hand so he won't be scared."

I cupped my hand around him gently and was surprised when he stopped struggling immediately.

We went back to the rock and sat down, each holding a beautiful bird in our hands. With his free hand, he took from his pocket a little bottle with a small brush attached to the cap. He held the bottle between his knees and unscrewed the cap. Then he gently applied the liquid to the birds' feet and unglued them from the branch. He placed the bird in the box and put the lid back on. Then he did exactly the same with my one. He waited several minutes to allow the birds to settle down and then reached in and took one out. I could now see it up close as my father held it gently by its' small feet. As it sat there on his finger, I was awed by its tiny size, no more than two inches long, yet so perfect. It had black and gold wings and an ivory colored beak. Its head was black and it had a red mask all around its eyes.

"This is a male," said my father, "We will keep him."

He placed the bird back in the box and took the second one out.

Looking closely at the bird he said,

"We must let this one go."

"Why do we have to let him go?" I asked sadly.

"Because this is a little female and she probably has a nest somewhere."

Not wanting to give up I asked,

"But how do you know it's a female."

"If you look really close you will see her red mask does not go all the way around her eyes. That's how you know it's a female."

"We must let her go as she may have chicks to feed." Then handing her to me he said,

"Now, you let her go."

I held her in my cupped hands and slowly opened them. At first, she just sat there looking at me until my father leaned over and blew gently on her feathers. Then, in an instant, she was airborne, her wings flashing black and gold as she circled us twice, then flew straight to the thistles.

We walked home contented that day, with our singing friend in the shoebox.

"We will have to keep an eye on your mother's cat from now on," warned my father, laughing. And I laughed too.

The Cultivation of a Canine

A Lesson on Handling Troublesome Dogs

I must stress upon the reader the fact that no animals were harmed in any way during the writing and re-telling of this story. It is true though, that the star of the tale was definitely shocked, awed and mesmerized not to mention puzzled, bewildered and befuddled. As you read, I am sure you will agree that the unruly canine brought it upon himself with his dogged actions towards my hapless father.

A sharp *whack,* delivered gently but firmly, to his snout stopped him instantly and with startled yelps he ran for the garden of his owners' house, cleared the fence with an Olympian leap, then crouched whimpering, under the hedge. That was the last time the neighbor's dog Spot, ever feasted upon my fathers' ankles. Spot was a black and white border collie who dwelt with his masters. They lived in the house on at the corner at the end of our row. Every day for a week my father Mal had to run the gauntlet as he steered his new red motorbike past the crouching canine. Spot lurked and waited patiently for the distinctive *vroom vroom* sound that told him his quarry was near. As his victim approached the corner, the stealthy cur would pounce and grab my father's leg. No amount of shaking could get him to loosen his grip, kicking and shaking just seemed to spur him on. Only when they got near to our house would he release his fangs and saunter back to his lair and wait for tomorrow when the fun would begin once more.

"Look what that savage did again," my father exclaimed, red faced and angry, as he dismounted and bared his chewed ankle and torn trousers. He had, on several occasions, diplomatically approached the mutts' owners, seeking a fair resolution to the dilemma. A half-hearted attempt was made to curtail his movements but this only entailed a feeble, *bad dog* admonition and an even feebler attempt to keep their gate closed and hope for the best. He quickly found an escape hatch and continued his assaults with unbridled passion. There was only one way in and out of the housing complex and realizing that he would encounter Spot every day my father decided that it was he or the dog. Something had to be done.

Later that evening as I came around the corner into our back yard I found my father sitting on an upturned milk crate whistling. He had the bottom half of an old broken fishing rod in his hands and removed the reel that was attached to it. The motorbike was on its kickstand and sat along the low garden wall. He sent me to the garage to get his saw that hung on a hook inside the door. He had tools everywhere but I could only use them when he was around.

"Too dangerous," he often warned.

"Can I have the reel, dad?"

"Yes you can, it's still a good one."

"Are we going fishing?" I asked, hopefully.

"Nope no fishing today."

"Aw." I said disappointed.

"Are you making something?"

"Oh yes!" He laughed, "I'm making a present for *Spotty boy*."

He took the saw and like a professional, held it up and with one eye closed, looked down its length making certain it was straight. Then he held the tip with his left hand, grasped the handle in his right one, bent the blade slightly, and brought his thumb down sharply. As he did this, a clear note rang out loudly, sounding like a bell. By bending and flexing the blade, he could produce several different notes. I was amazed every time he did this and couldn't wait until I was older to try it for myself. As he made the notes ring out, he sang a little rhyme,

"Spotty boy. Oh. Spotty boy
I have made a brand new toy.
It's not for fishing, no siree.
It's for your long snout, as you will see."

We both laughed heartily at this and he sang it again, louder this time. "What are you two laughing at?" asked my mother as she poked her head out of the kitchen window. She was cooking and the delicious aroma of frying bacon wafted out over the back yard and made me lick my lips. I sang the song for her and she started laughing too.
"Promise you won't hurt him, Mal," she pleaded.
"Ellen, I'm only going to scare him, don't worry," he promised and winked at me. He cut the rod and inspected his handiwork, waving it like a baton. "Perfect," he said and gave it to me to see it up close.
Then, he held both of his hands out, waved them, and inquired,
"Who will I leave these hands to when I am gone?"
I always laughed when he said this and could hear my mother laugh too, through the open window. It was the bottom end of the fishing rod with the soft, spongy, cork covered handle. He had shortened it to about a foot and a half in length and when I handed it back to him, he gave it a few practice swings. Satisfied with his creation he announced,
"We will test it out tomorrow."
Whistling, he then went inside the house.

The next afternoon I raced out of the school yard and ran to the park opposite Spots house. Sure enough, he was there asleep on the step as usual. As I sat on the grass waiting for the familiar sound of the motorbike, he sat up, yawned, scratched himself thoroughly, settled back down on the step and went back to sleep. I waited listening intently and after what seemed like hours, it happened. Spot heard it before I did. Suddenly, as if he was poked in the rear with a sharp object, he bolted upright, began howling, and started chasing around in circles. Then I heard it, *vrrrooom*. The sound was getting closer *vrrrrrrooooom*. Louder now. Spot stopped spinning and lay flat on his stomach just inside the gate, his tongue hanging, his ears fully erect and his eyes fixed. He was ready! Around the corner came Mal and out of the gate charged Spot, gnashing and snarling. As he lunged towards my father,'s leg the shortened fishing rod slid down from my father's sleeve as if by magic, and with one swift move, he tapped Spot gently but firmly directly on the nose, just between his eyes. As he did this, I heard my father say, "I'm sorry Spot but it's either you or me."

For what seemed an eternity, the dog was transfixed and seemed to be frozen in midair. He had a strange glassy, faraway look in his eyes and his hanging tongue flopped around wildly. It reminded me of the expression on *Wily coyote's* face in the roadrunner cartoons, just before the anvil hit him. His once erect ears now hung limply on either side of his mesmerized head. Dazed and befuddled he looked all around as if thinking,
"How did that happen?"
He was in shock and in that instant, his canine personality altered, forever. When realization finally dawned on him, he turned and ran yelping back across the road, leaped the fence and scampered under the hedge. Since the day of that fateful encounter with Mal, every time Spot heard the horrible sound made by my father's demonic machine he would freeze in his tracks and a haunted, worried look would appear on his doggie countenance. No matter where he was, he would scamper wildly for the shelter of his garden,

jump the fence and race for refuge and safety, under the hedge. Every day for good measure, as my father passed the neighbors' gate he would open the throttle wide and with several loud *vroooms* remind Spot to be a good doggie. Sometimes he would slow down as he passed and sing that little song in his mellow, tenor voice, just for Spot.

Clifton Fair

A Lesson on Speed

Mal arrived home one Friday evening as the long shadows were fading. I always knew he was on the way when I heard him whistling. As he rounded the corner, I saw that he was wearing his lucky hat, the one with the homemade flies stuck in the headband. He usually wore it at an angle down over his left eye, but anytime he was bent on stressing a point of view, he would level it and push it back on his head. Trotting alongside him on a leash, was a scrawny, spindly legged, black dog with a long snout. I was playing football on the green with my friends and ran over to our house when I saw him walking towards the gate.

"What's that?"

"This," he exuded, as he proudly presented his latest acquisition with a majestic sweep of his arm, "*this* is the next champion of Ireland."

Just at that moment my mother stepped out of our front door and with her hands on her hips queried, "Where do you think you are going with *that* thing?"

"This *thing*, as you call it, won the 800 yard sprint in Limerick city!" replied my highly insulted father.

"I don't care if it won the Grand National in the holy city of Rome. You're not bringing it into this house, that's for sure," she replied, turned on her heel, and went back inside.

Now, I knew that the Grand National was a horse race and was just about to correct my mother when I noticed my father shake his head rapidly from side to side and mouth silently, *No! No!*

"Best thing to do when a woman is angry is to bite your tongue," he had advised me on many occasions, and I remembered that advice and heeded it often, later on in life.

"Women," he muttered, under his breath. "You can't live with them, you can't live without them, and you can't shoot them!"

Then, with a tug on the leash, he and the dog walked, their heads bowed, around the side of the house into the back yard, with me following closely behind.

"What are we going to do now?" I fretted when we were out of my mother's line of vision.

He had tied the leash to the handle of the garage door and gone inside.

"Now," he announced, as he came outside waving a hammer, "we will build a kennel."

Then with a nod of his head towards the kitchen window, added,

"Then we will try and placate her majesty."

I looked over at the trembling hound and felt a twinge of pity as it stood there looking lost. It was a strange looking creature with sad eyes, the tail tucked tightly between its back legs. It didn't look much like a champion to me and I said so.

"Looks can be deceiving," said my father hefting the hammer in his right hand.

"What are we going to call him?"

"She already has a name. She is called *Clifton Fair.*"

Along the back wall of the garage, there was an unused space and my father decided to build the kennel there. We erected a platform using two by fours and plywood and set it about a foot off the floor. Next, we built a wall about six feet high, using the same materials and in the wall we inserted a door with a window in it. A thick bed of straw, laid on the platform, completed the sleeping quarters. And so it was, later that night the next champion of Ireland took up residence in 43 Rathview Park.

Early the next morning I found my father in the back yard stirring something in a large, black pot, which was sitting on top of a small gas stove. Clouds of steam were billowing all around the yard, like a thick fog, so thick you couldn't see in through the window. He had been to the butcher's shop on the square earlier, and bought some minced beef and a large bag of dog food from the grocery store.
"What's that for?" I asked, pointing at the cauldron.
"I'm making her breakfast," he replied nodding towards the kennel, stirring furiously. I caught a shadowy glimpse of my mother through the steamed-up living room window. She was looking at my father and had her hands on her hips again. I said nothing and walked over to the kennel and looked in. The champion was stretched out on the straw, asleep. She looked very relaxed and not at all nervous then. I opened the door, went in, and sat down beside her, as Mal prepared a breakfast for a champion.

The next morning the training regimen began. First, she was let out in the garden to run around and exercise, then she was brushed until her coat was shining. As Clifton Fair was her official name it was decided that, she needed a pet name and we all agreed that it would be Blackie. Every evening I would walk her for several miles and on Saturdays and Sundays. My father and I would take her to a large open field for a run. I would take her on the leash to the opposite end of the field and when my father gave me the signal, I would let her free. When he whistled and waved his hat Blackie would take off running at high speed toward him. Then it would be my turn to call her and when my father let her go, she would sprint across the field toward me, her tongue lolling. We would repeat this several times until she appeared tired, then we would head home. One Sunday as we were about to let her run, my father took a stopwatch from his pocket.

"Let's see how fast she is."

"Why do we have to time her?"

"Before we can enter her in a race she must be able to run at a certain speed." He was satisfied with her pace because the next day, Monday, he and I went to the race track in Dundalk, a town about 7 miles away, and entered her in her first race. The racetrack manager said he would send us a postcard letting us know the date and time of the next race meeting.

"No more running for her this week. She has to rest and eat well. We will walk her everyday only, to keep her supple."

"Do you think she will win?"

"I am not sure, this will be her first race and she must get used to racing with other dogs first, but you never know. At least we will try"

Everyone was excited about Blackie's first race and we planned that the whole family would go to the track. I walked her every evening for several miles and my father fed her a special, high protein diet every morning.

I woke with a start early on Thursday morning, a vivid dream still fresh in my mind. In it, I was at the race track sitting about half way up in the stand. Looking around, I saw a large clock on the wall above the food bar, the time was 7:15pm. I turned my head in the direction of the track and could see six large, colored, wooden boxes, lined up across the track. Each box was a different color and had a number painted on the flap in front.

The boxes were called *traps* and after walking the dogs once around the oval to familiarize them, the white coated *handlers* placed a dog in each box and closed the flaps. My father was standing at the rail, which ran all the way around the oval shaped, sand covered track, waving at me. I stood up just in time to see the electronic hare, which was attached to a metal rail about one foot off the ground, as it sped past the boxes.

The loud, excited yelps of eager dogs could be heard all around the track and suddenly, the flaps on the boxes sprang open and the six dogs burst forth and raced after the fake hare, their wild barking echoing. Everyone was on his or her feet by then shouting and cheering on their dog of choice hoping their one would win. Following his or her progress, I could see that each dog had a small plastic cover attached to its back. On the cover, a number matching the trap from which each dog had started from was clearly visible. Blackie's number was six and she ran so fast I had trouble keeping my eyes on her. I could hear my father shouting, "Come on six!" at the top of his lungs and waving his hat. Coming around the last bend the dogs were now at maximum speed, their slim bodies at full stretch as they lunged forward. With one hundred yards to go, number six, with a final spurt, raced along the inside, close to the rail and passed the other dogs one by one. She crossed the finish line two yards ahead of a brown dog who wore the number four. Blackie had won the race!

When I came home from school on Thursday evening, I found my father in the back yard. He was in a good mood and talking to Blackie. "Good girl, we will show them who is the fastest," he was saying, as he rubbed her all over with something from a lemonade bottle.

"What's that?" I said pointing.

Holding the bottle up he said, "This is *poteen*, pure alcohol, and good for her muscles." "What does it do?"

"It warms her, makes her supple, and loosens her up."

Blackie was just standing there and seemed to be enjoying all of the attention, she looked happy.

"Bring me my coat."

"Where is it?"

"In the garage."

When I handed him the coat he took a white postcard from the inside pocket and handing it to me said, "Here read this, it came this morning." *We are pleased to inform you that your dog Clifton Fair is entered in the 7:15 pm, race at Dundalk on Friday June 21st. She will start from Trap number six. Good Luck.* Trap six! I remembered the dream again and told my father about it. "Wouldn't that be something!" he laughed.

We left the house early on Friday evening in two cars. My father, mother, me and Blackie in one and my uncle Joe and sisters in the second. About a mile outside Dundalk, my father stopped the car along the roadside, got out and said, "Bring her out and hold the leash." He had the lemonade bottle in his hand, and after sprinkling the contents all over her neck, back and legs, he slowly massaged Blackie, all the while talking softly to her. "How does that feel girl, eh? This will make you feel good and you'll run faster than the wind!" We arrived at the track at six thirty and my father and I went straight to the weighing room, the others went to find seats. After signing Blackie in my father gave her to one of the handlers, then we went to the betting window to place our bets.

I had four pounds saved from doing my newspaper round and I bet it all on six to win and four to place. After that, I went to the viewing stand to wait for the race to start. I found a seat with a clear view of the track and saw my father as he made his way down to the rail close to the starting line.

The handlers were almost finished with their walk and as they came to the traps, my father turned and waved to me. The dogs were put in the traps, the hare sped past, the yelping dogs burst out at great speed, the crowd roared, and Blackie came racing along the rail crossing the finish line in first place. The brown dog, number four, came second. It was exactly the same as it was in my dream! On the way home, I sat in the back seat with a sleeping Blackie stretched out beside me. "How much did you win?" my father asked.

"Sixteen pounds."

"What will you do with all that money?"

"I'm going to buy a new collar for Blackie and a fishing rod for myself."

"Very good! And with my winnings, I will buy you a new reel."

My father made up a song about Clifton Fair and we sang it all the way home.

He told me later that first race was the most important one and when I asked him why he replied, "When I first brought Blackie home, many people told me I was mad, that I didn't know anything about racing dogs, that I was wasting my time. I felt that it was at least worth trying and even if she never won a race, at least I wouldn't have any regrets about it. Besides, look at all the fun you and I had training her."

Blackie went on to win many more races but it was that first one that we all remember.

John A. Brennan

Mass

A Lesson on The Importance of Faith

I wouldn't say my father was an overly religious man, but he did insist we all attend Mass on Sundays and church holidays. He also instilled in us a strong sense of right and wrong. Integrity was vitally important to him. I have to say he was not in any way a hypocrite as he always led by example. On the rare occasions that anyone of us would be foolish enough to do something he considered to be, beyond the pale, he would administer his tried and tested version of the not as yet invented *Ritalin*, that is, a sharp slap to the nape of the neck followed by a swift kick up the arse. This usually deterred any further infractions and ensured compliance to Mals' rules concerning co-habitation in 43 Rathview Park. I had no problem with any of this, in fact I enjoyed going to Mass on Sundays. I always got to wear my Sunday best and I also enjoyed the rituals, the robes, and the reverence of it all. The smell of incense would waft heavenward, and the choir would sound divine. When in my teens I migrated from the main body of the church up to the men's gallery. There I could ogle the girls enthroned in their Sunday finery, in the women's gallery opposite. It truly was heavenly to sit there, high up in what was fondly known as the viewing box, and take in the sights and sounds.

The fact that the Mass was said in Latin then had little impact on the pleasure, it actually enhanced the experience, as I didn't feel that I had to pay too much attention. I would make sure that the seat chosen was well out of my father's line of vision. He had excellent sight, hawk like, and for a time I believed that, he must have had a ring of spies watching my every move. He would sometimes conduct spot checks if he had any doubt that mass might have been skipped, or if he suspected inattention to the service. After Mass as we were seated in the kitchen having lunch, it was not unusual for him to enquire quietly from behind his newspaper,

"Who said mass today?"

That was an easy one. Even if mass had been avoided that day, I could always ask someone who had attended. Another favorite of his was,

"What was the sermon about?"

That one was a bit trickier, but still, the gist could be gleaned from a friend who had attended, and recited at will, thus avoiding a dose of Mal's version of *Ritalin*.

On Saturday evenings, confessions were heard to purge the sullied soul in preparation for the next days' rituals. A short set of small sins and misdemeanors would be memorized, easy to rattle off in the confession box. Every week they would be changed around so that the priest wouldn't become bored or suspicious. We always migrated to one priest in particular, Father Halfpenny. He was known for his rapid forgiveness of sins and his confessions lasted only half as long as the other two confessors. His penances were usually one our father and ten hail Marys' and even if one of the sins confessed concerned lurid thoughts about girls, the penance remained the same. Father Halfpenny was a saint in our eyes and understood the whole puberty thing, hormones, and all, and we loved him for it. In our eyes, he was already elevated to earthly sainthood. When he said Mass, the time was cut from the usual hour long to thirty minutes. Needless to say, his services was extremely popular and always packed and there was a waiting list for his confessions.

Once, a pious older lady complained to the Parish priest that Father Halfpenny must surely be leaving out parts of the Mass, as he was far too speedy with his delivery. She was asked to identify which parts of the ceremonies that she felt were missing, but since it was conducted in Latin at that time, she was stumped and therefore had to endure the short version.

She was the biggest scandal monger in the town. At Mass, as the time for receiving communion drew near, she would sidle like a crab to the end of her row, and with an intensity that only someone on the cusp of blessedness is endowed with, would wait for the precise moment that the priest elevated the *holy host*. As he raised his hands skyward, she would vault from her seat like an athlete and race to the altar rails with such speed and agility that we all believed we were witness to a truly miraculous event every Sunday. For a woman of her age she had the vigor and vitality of a sprinter, and was always first to reach the rails and the last to return to her seat.

If I had a dislike for any part of the religion regimen, and if I am perfectly honest, I would have to say that the family rosary was a bone of contention always. Every night at six thirty, without exception, my father led us all in saying it. No excuses would be tolerated; homework could be done later. Everything else took second place. It usually took around thirty minutes to complete and he had a very annoying habit of rattling his rosary beads as a sign that the ritual was about to commence. Everyone would kneel and take turns in saying a decade of the rosary. If a hapless neighbor should choose that moment to pay a visit, they too would have to assume the kneeling position and pray with the rest of us. For me, Thursday nights were always the worst. At seven o'clock every Thursday, Top of the Pops was on TV. It was a music show that aired and featured the top selling artists for that week. The Rolling Stones were guaranteed to be performing and they were my favorite band.

Whether my father was aware of the importance of this or not, I can't say for sure, but I noticed that the rosary always took longer to complete on Thursday nights. He seemed to say the prayers in slow motion with long drawn out *H-a-i-l M-a-r-y- F-u-l-l Of G-r-a-c e s* and more than once I am positive, I heard him mutter something about, long haired layabouts in the middle of the recitations. My way around this was to have my sisters, when it came their turn, speed up their replies and I would do likewise. The slower he became the faster we responded. I had learned this fast way from listening to Father Halfpenny, I think and in this way, I could usually get to see the last ten minutes or so, of the show. Some visitors would actually arrive just as the rite began, full of the Holy Spirit and eager to pray. Others though, would time their visit so that they arrived just as the last Hail Mary was being recited. As you walked along North street on the way to the church you would pass one of the many bars that seemed to be everywhere across the town. Even though the bars were closed on Sundays, the haunted looking, nerve wracked, early morning tipplers could be observed standing outside, their backs to the door, tapping with a coin the agreed code that would gain them admission. Once inside, a hair of the dog would be ordered, gulped down quickly followed by another and only then, could the previous night's antics be discussed, interpreted, and in some cases, re-enacted.

After Mass we would race out the door, clamber down the steps and jostle for pole position outside the church to watch the *angel parade*, then the sin list would start all over again. This was a very popular practice and very, very invigorating. Looking back on it all now, that was probably the most enjoyable part of all those sacred ceremonies.

John A. Brennan

The Swans

He glides across the smooth lakes' surface,
but she is nowhere in sight.
Stately he moves on ever through the night.
A moonbeam beckons to a hidden place
where once they did dwell.
Faster now, maybe she lays there,
and love again might they share.
But no earthly sign now, only pain.
Mute, and no sound escapes.
The reeds and rushes lay empty.
The archer with arrows more plenty,
has struck in her hearts' place.
He follows the fading silver beam upward
toward the eternal light.

The lake is quiet now, now that the swans have gone.
Once they sailed its wide surface, silent and free.
A ghostly presence is all that lingers on,
to remind us of what there used to be.
He searched for her, but alas, no trace, no sight.
Meshed together now, mid the moons' clear light
His last song silent sung, from deep within.
Then, merging slowly with the mist,
he fades from without.

The author's daughter, Joanne Brennan in Paris (1986)

Back When

But through it all there was the music.
Saving me, shielding me, and thrilling me.
Back When I was Jumping Jack Flash.
Strutting, swaggering, being Jagger and me as one.
Flippin' the switch. No one was gonna make a saint
out of me, that was certain.
Back when I was the midnight rambler,
seeking sympathy from the Devil, craving redemption.
Back when the Rolling Stones rocked London town and
then the world.
Back when Dylan was our prophet, the minstrel,
the piper at the gates, changing the times with his
goading sneers. "The times they are a-changin," he warned.
Back when Bob Marley, the seer, simplified it all,
showed us the pathway to one love, one heart.
"Let's get together," he said.

Flynn Family Wedding (circa 1965)

Back row (L-R) unknown guest, unknown guest, Mal, John's father, Vincent Flynn, Johnny Flynn, Pat hearty, unknown guest. Front row (L-R) Vera Flynn, Brigid Brennan, uncle Joe, Eileen Flynn, Mary Flynn and unknown guest.

The Brennan Family in Urker

Back row (L-R) Aunt Dolly, John Brennan, and his uncle Joe. Front row: sister Marion, cousins Mary, Jack and John's sister Teresa.

CHAPTER 5

On People

Biting One's Tongue

The bard of Avon, William Shakespeare once said,
"All the world's a stage and each must play his part."
How right he was! He knew, and tried to forewarn us that the moment you
step outside your front door you are onstage. No time for a dress rehearsal.
Break a leg! It matters little what transpired only moments before, whether
your long suffering spouse let it be known once again, that they are less
than satisfied with your conjugal performance, or the unwed apple of your
eye just announced she is having twins, you cannot show any of this to the
world. Why? Because you are and must be an Actor.
You must say, "Good morning," with a smile, to the first person you
encounter, no matter who it is. "How are you today? What a wonderful
morning."

Then you must be prepared to stand and listen if this person proceeds
to bend your ear and assault your senses for perhaps, a half hour or more.
You are and have to be, two faced. One that you see when you look in the
mirror and the other you present to the external world. It must be this way
otherwise you are inviting trouble. Your day will go down and your blood
pressure will go up from that very instant.

There is no doubt that you are going to meet nasty, aggressive
individuals in the course of your day. You can't avoid them. It is sadly, an
inherent part of human nature. Sometimes it seems as if many of them
actively seek you out. The only thing you can do is tailor your reactions to

their actions. I was taught this early in life by my father Mal, a past master. His method was simple. "Bite your tongue," he would say under his breath. He repeated this many times as I was growing up. Granted it sounds very simple, but I can assure you that with my Irish temperament, it takes years of practice. The biggest surprise to me after all of these years is that I actually have a tongue left to bite.

I can always judge my performance by counting the number of times during the day that I have bitten my tongue. In fact, I have become so adept that I start biting the moment I see certain individuals, even from afar. I have, on many occasions, clamped down tightly when just the mere thought of a certain person crosses my mind. Just to be on the safe side, I always bite my tongue before I step out of my front door. After a while it becomes part of the daily routine: shower, breakfast, dress, and bite.

This simple act sets the tone for the rest of day and serves as an important reminder. I have discovered that aggressive people feel justified only if they receive negative feedback. They seem to thrive on negativity, and only feel that their righteous indignation is warranted, if they get the anticipated reactions. What they really crave is a sparring partner. Biting your tongue will give you breathing space and time to absorb the individual's verbal assault. You will notice that their voice often gets progressively louder and some may even become quite animated. At this point, another bite may be necessary, maybe two. Do not, I repeat, do not, be tempted to whistle carelessly during the encounter, as this will only inflame the antagonist's passion, and in some cases it has been known to cause apoplexy. Eventually, this irate person runs out of steam and with their blood pressure elevated, turn, and storm off. At this point, in a low voice you calmly make the simple statement that resolves the issue. The practiced aggressive, will always give you a final over the shoulder rejoinder, as if they were ending with an exclamation point!

Then and only then is it safe to stop biting.

Most small towns have their fair share of characters, gentle souls that are considered to be different. They are sometimes referred to as harmless, and indeed they are but they always have a quickness of mind and are experts in the art of repartee. What they lacked in formal education they more than compensated for with their razor sharp wit. Children were always drawn to them as if they could sense their simplicity. It seems to me that the smaller the town's population, the more characters you will have. This was certainly true growing up in my hometown of Crossmaglen, County Armagh.

The Rent Man

Every Friday, Pete, the rent collector made the rounds. On a belt around his waist he carried a brown leather bag and in the breast pocket of his coat, a small, leather bound notebook for recording the payments. All transactions were conducted in cash only in those days. When you paid, Pete would put a tick mark next to your name. He was always well dressed, his black leather shoes highly polished and he wore heavy rimmed glasses. He had a very official air about him but could enjoy an occasional joke. He knocked on the door of a man named John one warm Friday morning.

"Good morning, John," said Pete cheerfully, as the door was opened.

"And good morning to you too, Pete," replied John, equally cheerful.

"That's a great morning."

"Indeed it is."

"No rain today."

"No, we had enough rain yesterday."

"Well, at least the farmers will be happy."

"I don't know about that, farmers are never happy."

Both men laughed heartily at the old joke, but when the merriment died down a serious look descended on both of their faces. Now it was time to get down to the important business of rent collecting.

"I'm here looking for the rent," said Pete, in his official rent collector's voice.

John looked at Pete seriously, scratched his head, shifted from one foot to the other, cleared his throat, and answered, "Well, why don't you come inside Pete, and both of us will look for it."

Pete did not laugh at this witticism and John got no tick next to his name that day. Maybe he would the following week.

The Wood Collector

Charlie lived alone in a small cottage just outside the town. Several times a week he could be observed out in the fields and hedgerows near his cottage as he gathered firewood. He had acquired one of those old fashioned perambulators, or prams as they were called, which he utilized as his mode of transport for the movement of logs, groceries and bags of coal, though not all at the same time of course. It had four large wheels and a black hood. When he had a heap of firewood gathered he would load it into the pram and wheel it home, whistling. You could always hear him coming before you saw him as the wheels squeaked noisily, as if they were complaining about being misused. He attached a bush saw to one side of the pram with some string and on the other side a small can of fresh milk hung on a hook.

Charlie, a tall man, around six feet four was a gentle soul who didn't talk much. Rain or shine he wore a long, black, bus driver's coat with no buttons and a hat with a shiny peak. In cold weather he kept his coat closed by tying a length of cord around the middle.

One day as Charlie was pushing his squeaky, log filled pram along the road, he was passed by one of his neighbors, riding a bicycle. James, lived in a small red brick house not far from Charlie's and was known locally as a jokester. He delighted in teasing Charlie every time they met, for some reason known only to him, and Charlie never retaliated. James and his wife had lived in their small house all of their married life and for medical reasons they sadly, could never have children of their own. As James rode past, and being in a particularly jocular mood that day enquired,
"Hey Charlie! Where are you going with the twins?"
Charlie, without breaking his stride, and tired of James' constant ribbing, answered sharply,
"Oh hello James, I was thinking of leaving one of them at your house,"
then, carried on with his journey nonplussed.
Embarrassed, James pedaling faster, was soon out of sight. He never teased Charlie again.

The Dealing Man

The *dealing* man can still be found in every market square in towns and villages across the world. Their nationalities and language may be different but the art of *dealing* always follows the same ancient ways.
Robert lived in a whitewashed cottage with a thatched roof at the lower end of the town and was a *dealing man*. He was very proud of the fact that he was part of a tradition that stretched back through the ages. Buying and

selling was his purpose in life and he took his work seriously. Haggling and arguing over the price of animals was an excitable and loud process. Turning on the heel and storming off in mock disgust after an insultingly low offer was made was a great part of the performance. Then, after being called back and offered a slightly higher amount, the dealing would resume. When the amount was finally agreed upon, both men would spit on their hands and slap each other's palms signifying the completion of the deal.

At days end the dealers would retire to their favorite bar and relive the day's events. *Dealing men* were expected to look the part at all times and they had a common mode of dress with only slight variations. Robert wore the *dealing mans* accepted attire of tan colored leather boots, tightly laced in a crisscross pattern and polished to a dazzling shine. His dark gray trousers had sharp creases and his white shirt was always spotless. A short, colorful, knotted, silk scarf adorned his neck, the ends tucked in the open shirt. His tweed jacket had a handkerchief in the breast pocket but it was only for show, as he never used it. In the lapel he wore either a rose or a carnation. A flat, matching tweed cap completed his wardrobe.

Robert bought and sold a variety of livestock including goats and donkeys and would parade his menagerie on the town square every first Friday of the month at the fair. Other dealers would come from far and near to trade and you could buy anything there from a chicken to a horse. Robert was standing in his usual spot one fair day trying to sell a donkey. Business was slow and by evening he had had no offers worth talking about and was beginning to tire. As he stood there he draped his arm around the donkey's neck and leaned against him for support. Sometime later, a squad of British soldiers trooped out from their barracks and proceeded to patrol around the town.

As they passed Robert they started laughing and making braying noises, mocking him and the donkey. One brave soldier stopped laughing long enough to enquire as he passed by,

"Sir, why are you holding your brother so tightly?"

Robert, unmoved and without hesitation replied,

"Well young man, I'm afraid that if I let him go, he might just run off and join the British army."

George

"Who am I going to leave these hands to when I am gone?"

This, from my father, Mal, as he waved his hands around proudly, upon completion of a task so simple a four year old could accomplish it equally well. The comment was directed toward George, as they stood in the garden beside our house, one sunny afternoon. George, a neighbor, lived with his brother and his wife just around the corner from us. He did not get along with his sister-in-law, and because of this spent a lot of time at our house. He had little or no formal education, but was an expert in the art of repartee. He was small in stature, around five feet tall, but with a large heart. He always wore a flat, peaked cap rain or shine, and would spin it around on his head, with the peak facing backwards, any time he was involved in manual labor, or if someone made him angry.

He and my father had spent the morning weeding between the rows of vegetables. It being a hot day, and because he had had a run in with Sara, his brother's wife that morning. George was not his usual, good natured self. Earlier, he had taken off his old, threadbare jacket and draped it over the fence, keeping the vest on. He rarely took it off, except when he took a bath, and that was an even rarer event. In the right hand pocket he kept a big, round watch on a silver chain, and though he couldn't tell time, it always had pride of place in the pocket. If anyone asked him what time it was, he would proudly take the watch out and hold it so the enquirer could read the time for him or herself. "That's the time there," he would announce and slip the watch back into the vest pocket. He received a small pension every week and after paying for his keep would buy whatever necessities he needed. He always bought a large bag of assorted sweets, which he would distribute among his faithful following of children. He didn't place much value on money and was content with just enough to live on. Once, he was asked, jokingly,

"George, will you take all of your money with you when you die?"

George, unhesitatingly answered,

"I don't know about that, but I do know that there are no pockets in a shroud."

When they were finished with the weeding, both men moved to the shade of the back yard, where the pleasure of a cold drink awaited them. My father had sent me earlier for a large bottle of *shandy*, a mixture of lemonade and beer, and I ran inside to get it.

"Who will I leave them to?" repeated my father, as he did his impersonation of the Cassius Clay shuffle, and waved his hands again, this time under George's nose. As they reached the back yard, George, hot and sweaty, and in no mood for my father's jocularity, snapped,

"Well Mal, I'll tell you one thing, you needn't leave them to me, because I'll just use them to wipe my arse!"

The Storyteller.

Mick was a storyteller. He loved nothing more than spinning a good yarn. Everyone knew his stories were made up but we loved listening to him because he always made us laugh. One Sunday after Mass as we sat on the stone wall that ran along beside the church, eyeing the girls, Mick came around the corner whistling. He was a tall, heavyset man with bright blue eyes and wore a black, wide brimmed, felt hat. He was always smiling and in his company you felt good. He sat down beside us and started to tell us his latest story.

"I went out for a walk last Sunday after Mass," he began.
"Where did you go, Mick," I asked.
"I walked across the fields behind my house," he replied.
"Did you see anything strange or startling?" queried someone else.
"It's funny you should ask that, because just as I reached the old apple orchard I saw a big red fox, walking towards me, licking his chops."
"Were you scared?"
"No, not at all, I think he was more scared of me. As he got closer I saw that there were feathers stuck around his mouth, and I knew he had just eaten some kind of bird."
"Did you know which kind?"
"Not then, but as I walked along, I followed the trail of feathers that led me to a small pond."
"Must have been a duck he ate."
"No, it wasn't a duck. I thought so at first, but I wasn't sure."
"Did you find out?"
"Yes I did. At the pond I started to look closely among the rushes and reeds."

"Did you find anything?"

"Yes, right among a large clump of rushes I found a pheasant's nest."

"How did you know it was a pheasant's nest?"

"There were seven blue speckled eggs inside and some pheasant feathers."

"What did you do then?"

"I took my felt hat off, put the eggs inside, and took them home. When I got home I put the hat under the stove to keep them warm, and wait for them to hatch."

"And did they hatch?"

"Oh. Yes! A week later every one of them hatched, and, you won't believe this," continued Mick, proudly," when they hatched, each one of them was wearing a small felt hat, just like mine!"

The Night Moths

My writing has always been greatly influenced by the Irish writers whose works have prompted me to pick up the quill and follow in their footsteps. I thank them all for their inspiration This is my humble tribute to WB Yeats.

I went down to the cool, dark woods,
when night moths were on the wing.
On earthly ghosts and raging floods
embraced my lonely pondering.
Moss clung fast to an olden tree,
near bank of river flowing slow
Salmon leap I smiled to see,
in silence, with a young moons' glow.
Fawn eyes bright, shone out at me,
from in the depths, and to and fro.
She licked my hand, while nestling free,
her tale to tell of the long ago.
She told to me, through cool night air
that time and space are here and now.
Spoke to me of a maid so fair,
with haunted look on her pale brow.
An apple blossom in her hair,
she haunts the woods in search of him.
To heal her heart and her love fair,
and cease the lonely wanderin'.
All at once near a white oak tree,
a girl in shimmering bright light,
came out and gently called to me.
Then both did meld, into the night.

John A. Brennan

Back When

Back when I had the love but ruined it
again, and again, naive, not knowing, unsure,
blissful in my ignorance.
Always looking for the one who could save my
soul, heal my body and mind. The other half.
The alter ego.
Back when I was too often the altered ego tripper.
Getting the kicks on route sixty six.
Back when Castaneda shared the teachings of Don Juan,
the holy man. Flying with the crow in the desert.
The black bird with the severe eyes. The messenger. Free.
Back when, down in Chaco, the dusty, sacred canyon,
among the pueblos, reading the petroglyphs, looking for
the Anasazi, the lost souls.
Back when peyote was the manna, opening the inner eye.
Looking, seeking what was right there under my nose.
Body and soul sundered, wasted, adrift.

Standing L-R John's cousin John Matthews, uncle Joe and John. Seated in the front are cousin Joseph Brennan, Lassie and cousin Jack Brennan (circa 1963)

John Brennan, Age 7

John's mother, Ellen Brennan Nee O'Connor.

Mal and John's uncle Joe

CHAPTER 6

On Coming of Age

Droppin' the Hand

If I was asked to name the most powerful thing in the world, I would answer the *hormone* without hesitation. Ounce for ounce, the pesky hormone has to be up there on a scale with nuclear fusion. Hormones entered my life with energy akin to an atomic explosion when I hit 14 years of age. Until then, I probably couldn't even spell the word. My main pastime back then was rambling through the fields, chasing rabbits with my black and tan colored terrier, Lassie, and watching the *Lone Ranger* on TV. I did have the frequent urge to pull a girl's hair then run off laughing. I still do, occasionally. Once, I crept up behind a classmate, lifted her skirt and was surprised to see that she had nothing on underneath. I remember thinking, isn't she cold? But that was about it. Nothing out of the ordinary. I only did it because I'd seen some of the older boys do it.

My introduction to hormones and their bizarre effects came from a classmate of mine as we sat in my backyard one day, after school. He was talking about his sister Mary, and told me that he would fix me up with her. "Fix me up, what does that mean?" I asked innocently. "You and her go for a walk, or something," he replied. "I don't want to go for a walk with your sister." I retorted, horrified. "Maybe you could take her chasing rabbits, she likes rabbits." That appealed to me, but I thought it strange that a girl would like running across fields, climbing over hedges chasing after rabbits. He leaned in closer, jabbed me with his elbow and sniggered, "Maybe she'll let you *drop the hand.* "Huh?" I said, puzzled.

123

I had heard the phrase used before by some of the older boys, and knew that it was always accompanied by loud sniggers. I also knew that it somehow involved girls. But as to what it truly meant, I was perplexed. "So, I'll tell her you'll meet her behind the wall, tomorrow after school." "OK," I said feebly. That night after dinner, and still puzzled, I asked my sisters what *droppin the hand*, meant. They looked at each other and shrugged their shoulders. They were as baffled as I was. I resolved to tell them, when I found out.

The next day, after school, I sat on the low stone wall at the bottom of the school yard, swinging my legs. I often used the yard as a short cut to the fields. There was a four foot drop on the other side, but I had done it many times. Lassie would just launch herself off it and land nose first, unscathed. We made a good team and she was already running across the field, yelping with excitement. I was just about to throw a stick, when I saw Mary come running around the corner. I slid off the wall, dropped the stick, and straightened myself up. Lord knows what would occur next. I was sweating. "Hello, Brennan," she called, waving.
"Hello Mary," I answered, and felt myself blushing.
"I can't stay out too long," she said, breathless.
"Why?"
"Because, I haven't done my homework, yet."
"Me either!" I boasted, proudly.

I climbed up on the wall then and she reached for my hand. I took it and was surprised at how small and soft it was. I pulled, she scrambled, and soon she was up on the wall beside me.
"Where are we going"?
"Over by the old ring fort. I saw some rabbits there yesterday."

At that, I did my best superman leap off the top of the wall, hit the ground feet first and then, to show off my superhuman qualities, did a cartwheel. I think Mary was impressed, at least she didn't laugh at me.

"How am I going to get down?"

"Jump, I'll catch you."

"Do you promise?"

"Don't worry, I won't let you fall."

She readied herself and after one or two false starts jumped; I reached out to catch her. Suddenly she was squealing, laughing, and grabbing for me. Two of the buttons on her blouse came off and her pale, fleshy breasts pressed against my face. I'll never forget how soft and warm they felt. As I maneuvered, somehow, my hand accidentally slid up her dress, right between her legs. We looked at each other for a long time, not daring to move. I was very conscious of how soft, warm, and moist it was there, and how good her breasts smelled. My knees started to shake and I felt sure that I was going to pass out. Much to my astonishment I discovered that I liked the way it made me feel.

"Brennan!" She gasped.

"I'm sorry, Mary," I stammered, red faced and quickly withdrew my trembling hand.

I felt sure that she was going to slap me, but she had a curious smile on her lips and was breathing heavily as I was. She reached in her pocket, took out a safety pin, and closed her dress. 'Girls always carry safety pins," she said and winked at me.

"I didn't know that you knew about *droppin' the hand*," she said laughing. So that's what it means! Finally I knew. I also knew that I could never tell my sisters. Leaning close she whispered, "I'll show you how to do it properly, but not here."

She took my hand then, and we walked off in the direction of the old ring fort. Funny thing is, chasing rabbits didn't appeal to me so much after that day.

The Rolling Stones…….. Geometry and Gravy.

"BRENNAN!…….. DID YOU CLEAN THE FRYING PAN WITH THIS?"

This utterance was roared by Mr. McMullan, the headmaster of the technical school, situated on the north corner of the square, next door to Peggy Martin's newspaper shop, in my hometown of Crossmaglen. As he uttered those immortal words, the veins in his neck throbbing dangerously, he flung the homework book in my direction with such ferocity, that it bounced off my desk, fell to the floor, and, still gathering momentum, skittered all the way to the end of the row, where it landed at the feet of Claire, a startled classmate. I arose shamefaced, from my seat in the front row, and with howls of laughter and loud braying sounds ringing in my reddened ears, I went to retrieve the cause of my mortification. As I bent down to pick up the book, I noticed three things. Firstly, the book was lying face up, and I could see two large red X's drawn viciously across the pages that contained my humble attempts at drawing triangles and trapezoids. Next, I noticed the cause of Archie's rage. A series of greasy stains that formed a curious pattern, not unlike a large capital *W*, were visible on both pages.

It is true that I was doing my homework during dinner the night before. We were dining on pork chops, mashed potatoes, peas and lots of my mother's famous homemade gravy. I must also confess that I was distracted by The Rolling Stones who were appearing on my favorite music show, 'Top of the Pops,' that night. I blamed Mick Jagger for the whole bloody mess, but I suspected Archie wouldn't understand, so I bit my tongue and said nothing. I remember wiping the stains off with the sleeve of my shirt, and felt sure that they would be a distant memory by morning. The third thing I noticed was that Claire had almost jumped out of her seat with fright as the book landed at the base of her desk. She had lifted her feet up and rested them on the rungs of her chair.

As I gathered the book I raised my head and discovered that I was looking straight up her skirt. The sight of her bright red panties made me gasp and gave me such a jolt that, as I stood up, I banged my head on the corner of her desk. She had seen my furtive peeking and immediately pulled her knees together and gave me a look of pure disgust. All of this only served to encourage the rest of the class to bray louder and laugh uncontrollably. I had the strange thought, as I stood there rubbing my aching head, that her red panties formed an almost perfectly shaped equilateral triangle, right there between her upper thighs.
I tell you, I learned more than one lesson that day.
One: Never watch the Rolling Stones while doing your homework. Two: Never eat mashed potatoes with gravy while doing geometry. And, most important of all, when you're looking up a girl's skirt, keep your head down and never let her see your eyes.

The Scapegoat : The rift

There must always be a scapegoat, a sacrificial lamb to assuage the guilt of others. Either this role will be accepted willingly or it will be thrust upon the chosen one. *It wasn't me*, is a commonly used phrase as the scapegoat is chosen. It surfaces early in the childhood years with a sibling shirking blame or trying to avoid responsibility. *He did it* is another favorite accusation leveled at the unfortunate, usually innocent victim. Sadly, this practice is not only confined to the formative years. It is an inherent part of the human psyche: in other words, it's in our genes. The practice of having someone else bear the blame, accept the guilt and by inference, suffer the punishment, goes back to ancient times and may even have been used by the first humans to inhabit the earth.

The earliest recorded mention of *scapegoating* comes from Syria in the 24th Century BC. An act of purification performed at a king's wedding involved a she-goat having a silver necklace hung around her neck and then driven out of the village, symbolically atoning for the sins of all of the inhabitants. The Hebrews used a more elaborate form of *scapegoating*. This ritual is believed to have started during the time of the *Exodus* from Egypt. The Israelites believed that the blood of their animal sacrifices during the year transferred all of their sins to the Tabernacle on the Day of Atonement. On that day the High Priest would confess these sins to a goat, which was cast out into the wilderness, absolving the Children of Israel of all wrongs.

We all, at one time or another will find ourselves in the position of the *scapegoat*. It matters little whether we are in fact guilty or not. Someone must *always* bear the blame. The earliest experience I had of this practice happened when I was almost 14 years old. One Saturday morning I had managed to elude my father and with Lassie my black and tan colored terrier at my heels, headed off for a ramble. My father would have a project lined up for the morning as usual but as I had earlier observed him digging in the back garden, from my upstairs bedroom window, I thought if I was fast and silent enough, I could escape. I usually looked forward to the times with my father, but sometimes it felt good to savor the freedom that rambling brings. So, grasping the leash from the door knob, I slipped silently down the stairs and out the front door. At the gate I rattled the leash and Lassie came tearing around the corner, her tongue lolling deliriously. I slipped it around her neck and putting my finger to my lips said *shhhhhh!*

Which direction should I take? I had to think fast, time was of the essence, for at any moment my father might appear. He had an uncanny way of appearing suddenly, like a spirit, as if he could read my mind. So, as often happens when making an instant decision, I invariably chose the nearest escape route and without further thought did just that. If only I had known what lay ahead. I raced across the green towards the row of garages on the opposite side of the park, the nearest point where I knew that once there, I would be hidden from view. At the rear of the garages lay the fields and that other magical world of nature.

"Don't tell him you saw me," I gasped at Mrs. Quinn as I raced past her. She looked up from weeding her garden and smiled as she said, "don't worry, I won't."Mrs. Quinn was a nice lady and had covered for me before. I was sweating now but almost there, just a few more yards. With a last glance over my shoulder I saw my father standing in the gateway. His hat was pushed back on his head and although I couldn't hear clearly I knew he was calling me back to the house. I ignored him and kept running.

Behind the garages was a secret space in the thick hedge and in a flash, with head bent, I tumbled through into the field. There on the lush, thick grass I lay panting, needing a few minutes to recover from the mad dash. Lassie looked up at me as if to say, "We did it again!"

Rested, I walked across the field with Lassie trotting ahead of me alert and watchful for rabbits. She had a passion for chasing anything that moved and at times I had to run to keep up with her. Suddenly, a blackbird disturbed by the snooping terrier, flew noisily out of a small whitethorn tree. I knew her nest was probably hidden carefully somewhere in the branches and ever curious climbed up and parted the leaves. Peering closely, *there it was!* I could see it but I would have to climb up a little higher to look inside. I stretched my arm and gripped a fat branch above my head, then hooked my foot on a lower limb and hoisted myself up. I was now at eye level and could see clearly, three little blackbirds with their mouths wide open. They had no feathers and their eyes were closed. I noticed several small pieces of eggshells spread around the bottom of the nest and so knew that they had hatched recently. I resisted the temptation to touch them as my father had explained that if I disturbed a nest the mother might abandon it. I stayed for a few more minutes marveling at the perfectly built nest and the ever hungry chicks inside; then, swung from the branch taking in the view from that different angle, hung there for a few moments, and dropped to the ground.

I saw Lassie off in the distance scampering up some gorse covered rocks. She knew there was a possibility of rousing a rabbit there as she had before. She had a long memory and always knew where to look. Sure enough a startled bunny bolted out from the bushes, eyes wide and ears fully erect. Immediately, a black and tan rocket burst forth and with excited yelps and barks, gave chase. The rabbit made a sharp left turn and took off over the hill with Lassie in hot pursuit. I scrambled up to the top of the rocks and watched the race from my vantage point, high above the grassy field. I could see the rabbits' white tail bob and weave first to the left and then to the right, then disappear in an instant through a hole in the hedge on the far side of the field. The black and tan terror flew through the same hole soon after. With both quarry and chaser now out of my sight I flopped down on the rock and prepared to wait for the hunters' return. It was then that I smelled the smoke.

It came ghostlike, wafting across the field from somewhere off to my right. I shaded my eyes with my hand to get a clearer view. In the next field were several large stacks of dried hay and one was in flames. A group of neighbors' children were running around the stack, hollering, playing cowboys, and Indians. They were from the upper end of the town and I remember thinking, *I'd better get out of here*, and was up and moving when I heard someone call my name and motion for me to join them. It was one of the children at the haystack. I shouted back and said I had to go look for my dog, and turned and walked off in the opposite direction. I whistled loudly knowing that Lassie would come and after a couple more sharp whistles, saw her running towards me, her tongue flopping wildly. I was worried now and knew that I had to get away from there.

As we approached the gate at the roadside a truck pulled into the field. It was the owner of the hayfield and his two sons. Without uttering a word they bundled me into the back of the truck and took off. Lassie ran barking after the moving truck that drove through the town and stopped outside our house. Now I was *really* scared. My father was in the garden tending to his plants and looked surprised as the truck drew up at our house. "Your son set fire to one of our haystacks," said the owner's younger son as he pointed off in the direction of the field. Everyone looked in that direction and sure enough thick black, smoke could be seen billowing above the rooftops and with it came a dreadful sense of impending doom.

"I didn't do it I swear," I blurted out as a cold, clammy sweat crept over my entire body.

"It wasn't me, I didn't do it," I repeated, quaking with fear.

"If it wasn't you, then who was it?' demanded the owner angrily.

Therein lay the moral dilemma. I did know who they were but also knew that I could never name them. No-one likes a tattle tale. So, in that instant, I became the sacrificial lamb and would have to bear the blame alone. My father had to pay for the loss and I worked off the cost over the next year by doing odd jobs after school and a paper round in the mornings. What upset me most of all was the fact that my father did not believe me. From then on the relationship with him became noticeably strained and we became distant. Many years later the perpetrator admitted to one of my sisters that it was him and not me who had lit the fire, but the damage had been done. Looking back now, I believe that was the day I grew up.

The Training Center

A year after the incident in the hayfield I left home. I had registered for a one year course at the College of Technology in Belfast, as a first year apprentice carpenter. It was September 1964 and I was fifteen. This meant I had to live in subsidized housing Monday through Friday but could go home for the weekends if I chose to. I arrived in Belfast on a Sunday afternoon, and found the city a vast change of environment compared to the rural life I had led up to then. It was my first time away from home and I was ill prepared and felt lost, thankfully, those feelings soon passed, as I became part of the everyday hustle. The course offered board and lodging as well as a stipend of three pounds a week. From Monday to Friday I attended classes daily and went home on most weekends. The college was situated at the bottom of the Falls road close to Smithfield market. There, in a classroom with fourteen other boys from all areas of Northern Ireland, I began to learn the fundamentals of working with tools and wood.

I was familiar with basic tools from watching my father work on his various projects, but they were nothing compared to the array laid out before me in the college workshop. Mr. Kilpatrick, our teacher was very knowledgeable and patient with us as we struggled to comprehend. After showing and explaining to us the various tools needed for working with wood he would test us regularly by holding a tool up and ask, "Who can tell me what this is?" If we recognized it we would answer in unison, "It's a plane, sir." Then another "What is this tool called?" Again we would answer, "A chisel sir." By the end of the first month we were well acquainted with all of the different tools. We learned about angles and the different joints used to affix one piece of wood to another. Holding two pieces of wood aloft he would enquire, "What is this joint called?" If we knew we would answer aloud, "A mortice and tenon sir." Then raising two more pieces would ask, "and this one?" again if we knew, we would answer, "a half Lap sir." Or "a dovetail sir" depending on which one he was explaining. He repeated these lessons until we knew every joint by sight. We were given written tests each month and we were taught how to use set squares, protractors, bevel squares, the three foot ruler and the roof square. I was fascinated by all of this new knowledge and was impatient to start my first project.

One Monday morning, after three months of instruction, as we sat at our desks Mr. Kilpatrick announced, "Today we are going to start making the most important item that you will need as a carpenter." We all

133

looked at each other wondering what it could be. "You are going to build your toolbox." We went with him to the woodshop and there he showed us how to select the different sized boards that we would need. He showed us how to *eye* each one to make sure it was straight. The toolbox was the first thing I made with my own hands and I was very proud of it. I vividly remember the feeling of accomplishment and the wonderful sense of creativity as I slowly measured, cut, and assembled those bare wooden boards. I constructed it using Parana pine, the hardest of the softwoods. It had space for all the tools I would need. It was thirty six inches long, eighteen inches tall and nine inches deep. It had a drawer for a square, chisels, ruler, a Yankee screwdriver, marking gauge, saw set and of course, a carpenter's pencil.

I built it using dovetail joints and strong glue and it would last for many years. In the bottom there was room for a hammer, two Stanley planes, a sharpening stone, and a small tin of oil. Inside the lid was where I kept my American Diston handsaw, the best handsaw on the market at that time. I installed metal protectors on each of the corners, fitted a sturdy lock on the top, and attached a leather strap handle, which made it easy to carry. I gave it two coats of black paint and then it was ready. It was a basic tool kit but enough to get me started. My plan was to buy one new tool every week when I went home. One weekend my father bought me the wooden three foot ruler, a square, and the carpenter's pencil.
"These are your most important tools, and always remember, measure twice, cut once."

My Uncle Joe gave me a Stanley smoothing plane. My mother gave me the money to buy a hammer and a saw. The rest I purchased on credit from Jack Cumiskeys hardware store and paid it off every weekend when I came home from the city.

After finishing my first year in the Training Center I, along with two other boys, was placed in Harland and Wolff's shipyard as second year apprentices. We, being Catholics, felt some trepidation as the shipyard was well known to employ a majority Protestant labor force, which was very anti-Catholic. Because we were part of the Government subsidized training program, they had no choice but to employ us. The first morning as I walked into the spacious, carpenter's workshop I saw a large sign, painted in letters two feet tall, high up on the back wall of the workshop which read, NO POPE HERE. Several British flags adorned the walls and other signs, read, GOD SAVE THE QUEEN. It was an unnerving experience and as the knot in my stomach tightened, I wondered if we would survive. *It's only for a year* we told each other later that day, as the three of us sat together at a table in the canteen having lunch. We had to sit apart from the rest of the workers, for our own safety I am sure, but we felt alone and outnumbered and were scared during that whole year. We were constantly harassed and roughed up and had to rely on our wits and brawn to survive. Name calling was a daily ritual and taunts of *Fenian Bastards* and *Catholic Pigs* were leveled at us in efforts to get us to retaliate. I remembered my father telling me prior to going to Belfast, "You must keep your wits about you in the City. You are going to be mixing with many Protestants and they will not be very friendly toward you. Keep your head up and don't hate them as they hate you, be wary of them, fear them, but don't hate them." I must confess, it was hard to follow that advice sometimes, but for the most part I did. Even today, after all that has transpired through the years, I still don't have the capacity to hate anyone.

It was now August 1966 and already the Civil Rights Committees were organizing. Catholics were discriminated against in most areas including housing, employment, education and non-property deed holders

135

could not vote. This practice was a direct throwback to the reign of king James 1, the English monarch whose desire in the 1600's, was to eradicate Catholicism. In late August 1966 the Ulster Volunteer Force was formed. It was set up as a paramilitary group whose sole aim was the eradication of Catholics. Soon after their formation the UVF burned many Catholic homes forcing whole families to flee for their lives. Intimidation by Protestants was rife and Catholics going out, especially at night had to be extra vigilant as beatings were common. I was beaten badly one night as I made my way home from visiting my cousins who lived close to Queens University. Not knowing, I had made the fatal mistake of taking a shortcut down Sandy Row, a Protestant enclave, and was set upon by a group of drunken youths. Thankfully, I survived and was glad when the day came that I completed the course. I was relieved that the ordeal was over and looked forward to going home.

The violence directed toward Catholics escalated to a fever pitch in 1968 with the first Civil Rights march in Derry City. The battle of the Bogside in Derry on August 12 1969 led to the deployment of British troops to Northern Ireland later that same year and full scale war ensued that lasted almost 30 years. In 1970, my hometown was thrust to the forefront of what had become an armed struggle for survival and lasted for almost thirty fearful years.

The Construction Site

When I arrived home, having finished my first two years in Belfast, my father approached Patrick Rogers, a local contractor and asked him to hire me as a third year apprentice. I worked with them for two years and learned the practical fundamentals of carpentry.

Rogers and sons were local contractors who built houses and schools. One of the great things about them was that they hired mostly local labor. The founder of the company was Patrick Rogers Sr. a tough, no nonsense individual who had spent many years as a young man in the USA. When he returned to Crossmaglen he brought with him both new ideas and tools that nobody had seen or heard of before. It could be said of him that he was an innovator ahead of his time. At 7:15 am, on a cold January morning I arrived at the construction site, carpenter's toolbox in hand, ruler in my back pocket, and a pencil behind my right ear. Twenty new houses were being built and I was excited and eager to start work. Snow had fallen the night before and covered everything in a clean white blanket. The official start time was 8:00am, so until then we huddled around the small gas stove that sat in the middle of a tin covered hut, making breakfast. The hut doubled as the canteen and storage shed on the site at Creggan, a small village one mile outside the town of Crossmaglen.

Gerry Rushe the carpenter, his brother Felix the bricklayer, Paddy McNamee the plumber, Paddy McAneaney the electrician, John Foley the laborer and me. Foley was showing me how to open a can of Campbell's soup using a hammer and wood chisel, then how to place it on the stove to warm it up. He also directed me in the fine art of tea making. His method was simplicity itself, put tea leaves in an empty milk bottle, add sugar and boiling water, shake the shit out of it and, voila, instant tea. Gerry was saying something about sending me to look for sky hooks and a glass hammer when a loud, clang, made me jump with fright off the upturned bucket that I was using as a makeshift seat. Two more clangs followed in quick succession. What surprised me was that no one else seemed to notice the racket, and carried on laughing and joking. It being my first day on the job as an apprentice and, green as I was, I flinched with every clang. To me it sounded as if we were under attack. The others looked at me, then at each other, and it was decided that I should go outside, and see what was making all the noise.

Being new, and eager to make a good impression on these learned individuals, my teachers in the fine art of building site etiquette, I got up and went to the door. As I opened it, I became aware of a sudden movement off to my left and watched in horror as John Rogers, the site foreman, lobbed a rustic, red brick in my direction. My first reaction was to duck my head, as the projectile came toward me in a descending arc, and with a loud crash, bounced off the tin roof, and landed in the snow, inches from my feet! "Its' 8 o'clock boys, time for work."
I could hear the roars of laughter from inside the canteen and at that moment wondered if I had perhaps made a wrong career choice.

Wood

The smell of freshly sawn timber always conjures up for me, an immediate vision of the land in which the tree was grown. In a strange way the tree comes alive and takes on a life of its own. Once its scent is released the magic begins. The humble pine, once I cut across its knotty grain, the strong, clean scent automatically transports me to the cool forests of Scandinavia. There, in the deep snowed forests, growing in the cold, crisp air, they tower majestically upward, reaching. The Archangel pine from that cold, bleak expanse of northern Russia, has a very subtle aroma, has no visible grain, and is as white as the snows of Siberia. Cutting through a plank of hard oak, and inhaling its strong earthy smell transports me to the lush forests of England, and I can almost envision Robin Hood hiding from the wily Sheriff of Nottingham amid the thick, sprawling branches. Mahogany always brings me to the Brazilian rainforest and the vast, steaming Amazon jungle, where it grows in magnificent profusion. The sweet, sensual, aromatic Rosewood from Madagascar, the African sister island to the Galapagos, always reminds me of guitars and other stringed instruments from which the fret boards are made. There is no doubt that I love the smell of wood. Working as a carpenter, the greatest feeling of all was when I entered an empty house that the other tradesmen had just finished. The rooms bare and the smell of fresh plaster strong in the air always made me feel that I was being presented with a blank canvas. In a week, my efforts would transform the bare space into a beautiful, new living area, and I was always proud of that accomplishment. I spent thirty years working as a carpenter and never lost the love for it.

Bobby

A tribute to a kindred spirit, a poet, soldier and
much braver man than I. Bobby Sands
died after sixty-six days without food or water
on hunger strike, for something he believed in.
5/5/81

The stone cold slab bruised hungry bones,
as he lay on the floor all alone.
His life ebbed nigh, but his spirit held high,
soon he would feast with his own.

The visions he saw, the hope that he felt,
would never be taken by force.

His will was complete, his heart, one last beat,
now the *way*, he would lead to the source.

Asking, "Why, oh why did you have to die
on this accursed foreigner's floor?"
Saying, "It has to be me, so it will not be you,
Now, I'll go and throw open the door."

The piper's lament was heard in wide space,
as the warrior was laid in his grave.
The lark soared high in a sorrowful sky,
as he left us to join with the brave.

Photo courtesy of Wikipedia Commons.
http://en.wikipedia.org/wiki/Bobby_Sands

Back When

And always Plato, drilling me, showing me, guiding me,
pushing me, but I in my throes always knew better
and blindly rushed headlong, frantic, toward my
blurred, unreachable horizon. Not knowing then that
'You can't always get what you want.' Not realizing then that
I didn't know what I wanted. With the mentality of the lemming.
Breaking on through to the other side. A Savage savant.
Heedless, arrogant and lost.
Back when I courted the stray cats, the blues, and the
honky tonk women and ignored Leonard.
What the fuck did Cohen know about love and suffering and
pain and heartache anyway, with his burning violin bullshit
and the end of love crap? Jimi Hendrix burning the strat!
He was my man! The highway child. The voodoo man in
the voodoo lounge. Merciless and mercifully dead before
his time, gone in a purple haze of glory.
"Hey Joe, where do you think you're going
with that gun in your hand?"
Back when Jim Morrison stormed the psyche with his sultry voice
and set us ablaze.
'Keep your eyes on the road and your hands upon the wheel,' he sang.
Then, left us for Paris high and the left bank and Sacre Couer
on the hill and Pere Lachaise in the valley.
The philosopher poet. The lizard king. Mr. Mojo risin.'

John's family at 43 Rathview Park. (1968)

CHAPTER 7

On Why I Came to America

I was asked to write something with an uplifting theme on the subject of the USA, by a friend and publisher Mr. James P. Wagner for inclusion in his Local Gems Press anthology titled Freedom Verse. Mr. Wagner's goal was to ensure a copy of the anthology got into the hands of every service man and woman as a way of thanking them for their unselfish efforts in protecting our great country. I was honored to do so as it afforded me the opportunity to express my thoughts on the subject. James, like me and so many others are sick and tired of the many naysayers and begrudgers who are quick to denigrate their own country especially if it appears to be seen as somewhat lesser, by her counterparts upon the world stage. What the USA needs at this point in history is for her sons and daughters to rally around and support her no matter what.

Freedom from Fear

The massive blasts of the four homemade, two-hundred-pound mortars, launched from the rear of a commandeered, flatbed truck, reverberated and shook the buildings throughout the town as they hit their target with deadly precision. Thankfully, all residents living in the immediate area had been warned in advance of the pending operation. This was the usual practice of the Irish Republican Army prior to military engagements. The night sky was set aglow with eerily brilliant domes as each shell exploded. The windowpanes in the houses closest to the target disintegrated into glinting shards, propelled hundreds of feet into the air by the huge shockwaves, deadly fingers of death for anyone unfortunate enough to be caught in their path. Roof slates cracked, loosened, and slid to the ground, laying shattered in broken piles in the street. Jagged, grotesquely twisted metal chunks of a Wessex helicopter, blown to pieces as it sat on its landing pad, whizzed through the night sky, landing in dozens of locations, some as far away as the cemetery, five hundred yards distant.

Heavy, rattling M60 machine-gun fire opened up from several vantage points, the armor-piercing tracer bullets glowing, as they coursed through the night air toward the British army barracks, striking, then ripping through the barrier walls. Automatic rifles sprayed the large observation post on the Square, ensuring those inside stayed there. In less than ten minutes, it was over. A hushed silence enveloped the town; all was quiet and still. The troops inside the joint Army/Police base did not venture outside for several hours. By then the volunteers had merged back into the Irish night and were long gone. This was life in my hometown of Crossmaglen, County Armagh, for almost thirty years.

Brendan Behan, a fellow Irishman, rebel, and Seannachie (storyteller), while living in the Chelsea Hotel in New York during the spring of 1963, wrote "To my new found homeland: "The man that hates you, hates the world!" I agree with Brendan. I was forced to leave Ireland for economic, religious, and political reasons and where else would or could I go? There was only one place that would accept me and welcome me as one of their own. Like Brendan Behan and his namesake predecessor, Saint Brendan the navigator, I too followed the long line of roving Irishmen and came to America. My journey was made much more comfortable, courtesy of Aer Lingus, our national airline.

As I waited for a taxi outside the international terminal at JFK airport and with the warm summer sun caressing my face, I was in a dreamlike state. Northern Ireland and the savage war, which had raged there for thirty years, were consigned to that other world I had now left behind. Almost immediately I sensed something profound had taken place. In that instant I was different. I felt lighter somehow and totally free. I was astonished when I realized that the deep-rooted monster, *fear*, was gone. I stood there unafraid for the first time in thirty years. Now, in America, my sanctuary, there would be no more running scared. No more armed soldiers stopping and searching me. No more house raids in the wee hours of the morning. No more beatings with rifle butts and arrests. No more gun clicks. No more being dangled from helicopters. No more coercion to become an informer. No more hunger strikes. No more attending funerals of young men and women, pacifists turned into reluctant soldiers. No more *fear*. *That is what America gave to me … freedom from fear.*

So, to the armies of naysayers, the legions of doubters and the countless ingrates I say, "Take the ferry ride to Liberty Island, walk to the feet of the lady with the torch, get down on your knees and read those treasured words inscribed on the plaque—digest them thoroughly and when you have done that, go out into the world and *live* them."

"Give me your tired, your poor,
your huddled masses yearning to breathe free,
the wretched refuse of your teeming shore.
Send these, the homeless, tempest-tossed, to me,
I lift my lamp beside the golden door!"

Crossmagalen Square (circa 1942)

Park Avenue.

In the glorious summer of 1993 I lived on Park Avenue in Manhattan. By all accounts, I should not have been, as earlier that year what I wanted to do was considered *impossible*. Completely out of the question! The good news is that there is a secret hidden in the word *Impossible* that only becomes visible after you split it into two words. When you do that you get two new words, *Im Possible*. My father Mal had shown me how to do it many years ago. He thankfully, also warned me about the naysayers. "The naysayer will give you a hundred reasons as to why you *can't* do something but not one reason why you can." His advice was to let them have their say, then redouble my efforts. "Their favorite word is *impossible* and they will use it frequently, listen to them and you will regret it," he added. One of the many phrases used by the naysayers the day I broached the subject of the possibility of managing an apartment building in Manhattan was a shocked, "That's preposterous! Are you out of your mind?"

I had naively asked my cousin Tom, who, with his three brothers, were in the building management business as high end Superintendents on Fifth and Park Avenues, some of them for thirty plus years. "That is impossible," he sputtered, shaking his head emphatically from side to side. "Dick," he called to his younger brother, "come here and listen to this guy!" "What?" asked Dick as he shuffled over to where we sat in the kitchen of Tom's apartment on Fifth Avenue, "Tell him what you just told me," said Tom, still looking at me as if he thought I was deranged and in need of psychiatric attention. "I would like to get into the building management business, like you guys," I repeated. Dick looked at me slack jawed, then at his astonished brother. "Are you out of your freakin' mind?" he exclaimed, dropping his donut on the floor.

"Are you serious?" he gasped, incredulous, as he bent down to pick it up. "It can't be all that difficult, and I thought that maybe with all of your connections and friends in the business you could maybe help me get started." "That is a complete impossibility. It can't be done. Totally out of the question," Harry, another brother exhorted as he upended his cup and stained the expensive red carpet with coffee. "Stick to carpentry, it's what you know," was the advice from Joe, the oldest brother, then he went back to sipping his Jack Daniels. The consensus among the extended family could be stated as, "You just can't do something like that. You must be crazy!" Then, with an exasperated "It's never been done before" attitude, they threw their collective hands up in the air and shook their puzzled heads. Not one offered any positive advice, only negative. I was disappointed by their responses and felt that they were being deliberately unhelpful. They truly believed that there was something seriously wrong with me.

Right then I *knew* that I was on the right path. It's been my experience that if everyone thinks your idea is doomed to failure then you are definitely on the right track. So, I could either scrap the idea altogether or heed my father's advice. I chose the latter. Maybe I was destined to remain a carpenter for the rest of my life. Maybe they were right and I was mad, after all I was Irish and had often heard the derisive term *mad Irishman* used. There's absolutely nothing wrong with being a carpenter. There once was a famous one from Galilee and one of my favorite actors, Harrison Ford was one before he decided to hone his other, untapped skills. I loved working with wood, especially hardwoods like Teak, from the Amazon rain forest, an exotic that oils itself or aromatic Rosewood with its' beautiful, tight grain.

When I built my first Grandfather clock I used the almost sensuous American, Black walnut with its long swirls and tight curls. Even the humble Pine has a strong, heady scent and can instantly transport you to the depths of a cool forest if you use your imagination.

I made a good living for twenty five years as a carpenter and designed and built my own house using the beautiful Brazilian mahogany with its' burled grain for the doors and windows. I had a lot of experience in all phases of construction and ran my own small company for many years, I just wanted to do something different. I was honest and could be diplomatic when dealing with people. I felt that these skills would be a great advantage to any prospective employer. When it came to managing residents, staff members, and contractors I knew I would make a good building manager. I kept thinking that there must be a way and so I determined to redouble my efforts. There was a way and I found it when I discovered night classes. What a wonderful concept! Work a regular job during the day and study at night. It would be difficult, but I felt that it could be done.

For six grueling months I worked as a carpenter during the day and attended classes four nights a week. At the end of the training course I had the required licenses and after putting my resume together, was ready to pound the pavement. I acquired a list of most of the real estate management companies in Manhattan and set out to distribute my resume. One month after that I was called for an interview. A meeting was arranged with the Board of Managers of a residential apartment building on Park Avenue. The meeting was held in a large, ornate living room in the penthouse apartment. The board comprised of nine individuals and was similar to sitting for nine interviews all at once.

It was a nerve wrecking experience at first but as the interview progressed I started to feel more comfortable and confident.

The board president asked, "If we decide to hire you, can you tell us how you would approach managing this building, its residents and staff, Mr. Brennan?" I replied, "The same way that I manage my life sir, I will use what I call the three *F* principles." "Can you explain what you mean by that?" asked another board member. "I will be *Firm, Friendly,* and *Flexible*," I replied. They seemed to be impressed with my reply and said that they would be in touch with me. With that, the meeting was ended. I received a phone call from the management company a week later and was told that I was being offered the position! I was hired and two weeks after that I took up residence. It all happened so fast and I couldn't believe my good fortune. I was going to live and work on world famous Park Avenue! Although I didn't realize it then, I had entered shark infested waters but still enjoyed many satisfying and fulfilling years on wonderful Park Avenue.

Sitting on my couch one evening about a week after moving in, I noticed two pairs of inquisitive eyes peering in between the slats of the window blind. I opened my front door and there on the sidewalk stood my cousin Tom and his friend Breen, looking sheepishly uncomfortable. They had heard an unbelievable rumor and were compelled to verify if it was really true. I believe that was the day of their conversion from naysayers to believers. It was also the day that the sharks began to circle. To this day, they still scratch their addled heads and wonder,
"How did he do it?"
Well, now they know.

Another regret put to bed dad.

The author at his Park Avenue apartment (August 2001)

The Firefighter

I often find myself thinking about my cousin Michael Brennan. He was a firefighter assigned to the *Pride of midtown* fire house in Manhattan. I first met him in 1990 soon after I arrived in New York City and was immediately impressed with his wonderful sense of humor and the way he made me feel truly welcome. He had the unique qualities of physical strength coupled with childlike gentleness. I sensed a good soul. Always jovial, he had a ready smile and a sharp wit. His greatest desire was to become a firefighter. When he finally realized his ambition his sense of pride was all consuming. He seemed to walk just a little taller and his stride appeared to be a little bit longer. On the morning of Sept.11 2001 he responded to the call of duty like so many of his comrades, and made his way back to Manhattan. Earlier, he had completed his previous night's shift and was having breakfast with his mother and sister at home in Sunnyside, Queens, when the phone rang. The call was for Michael. He listened to the voice on the other end, hung up the phone, turned to his mother, and said calmly, "Mom, I have to go." He never came back home.

I stepped out from my apartment on a glorious August morning and was greeted by the aroma of the plants and shrubs in the flower beds that ran the length of the Avenue. The heady scent took my breath away, as it always did. The trees were in full leaf and the sun was warm. I waved to Jim the doorman and motioned for him to straighten his hat. Jim was a good doorman but had a habit of wearing his hat pushed back on his head and slightly tilted, which is a no-no for a Park Avenue doorman. As I walked to the corner I barely noticed the blare of the two way traffic or the impatient honking of the cab drivers as I stood there enjoying the moment. The low rumble of a Metro North train heading uptown underneath the Avenue barely caught my attention. I was thinking how fortunate I was to be living in that great neighborhood. The sanctuary of Central Park was not more than two blocks away and from the moment I stepped inside, the city disappeared, the noise faded and the magic would begin. I normally used the entrance beside the Metropolitan Museum and would make the Egyptian obelisk the first stop on my rambles.

Suddenly, my reverie was interrupted when I was grabbed from behind in a bear hug, lifted up in the air and told, "Aha! I've got you now you Irish Mick." I knew right away that it was Michael as bear hugging was his favorite method of greeting. I would not have been surprised if he hugged real bears, he was burly enough, and I am sure he had many opportunities to do so as he loved the outdoors lifestyle.

"Sorry to wake you up," he said laughing and when he finally decided to put me down we talked for a while like old friends. He spoke about his uncle Joe who had recently returned to Ireland and we talked about our Irish heritage and of course women. I cracked an old, familiar joke about how 'fast women and slow horses' had always been my downfall and he roared laughing and added, "Don't forget the bad whiskey." Isn't it strange the things that we remember later?

He always laughed at that joke even though I must have told it a hundred times. He was like that. We chatted for more than an hour and as he was about to leave I asked him a question that had been on my mind for some time but never got around to asking. I said, "Michael, of all the careers at your fingertips why on earth did you pick one of the most dangerous when you could have chosen the one that the rest of the family follows?" I was referring to the fact that many of his relatives, including me, were building managers. He paused for a split second, looked me directly in the eye and with matter of fact seriousness answered, "Cousin, maybe one day I will have to come into your building and carry you out." His answer simple yet so profound, confirmed everything that made Michael one of those special beings we are fortunate to meet in this lifetime. He was one of those rare breeds who would, literally, lay down their lives to save others. He truly did lead by example and showed us all that actions do indeed speak loudest.

Three weeks after that black day in September, I was sitting on my couch with my daughter who was staying with me for a few days. The topic of conversation was Michael. His body had not yet been found and we were waiting anxiously for news. Ever since the dark, fateful day of his disappearance I kept a lighted candle on my coffee table. It was an old Irish custom meant to welcome home anyone parted from their loved ones. As we sat there talking quietly, a sudden blast of cold air swept across the room and extinguished the candle flame. Joanne and I noticed it at the same time and quickly looked at each other with open mouthed surprise. No more than two minutes later the phone rang. The voice on the other end informed me that Michaels' remains had been recovered from the rubble of the twin towers.

I am so glad that I got to meet Michael and get to know him, if only for a few short years. If I hadn't, I'm certain that it would have been one of those regrets my father had warned me about all those long years ago.

Firefighter Michael Emmett Brennan

John A. Brennan

The Long Eared Visitor

"A dripping faucet is not an emergency, Mrs. Crabtree."

The phone had rung earlier that Sunday morning rousing me from a deep slumber. I let it ring, as I knew the answering machine would pick up. It was my day off and believe me in my line of work, time off is precious. I manage a fifty family apartment building on Long Island and am responsible for the smooth day to day operation. Easy, you might say, but you realize that along with the regular skills needed you must also act as a psychiatrist in residence. I drifted back to sleep and was awakened minutes later by the incessant ringing of my apartment doorbell.

"Hell!" I muttered as I got up and reached for my bathrobe.

Rrrrrring. Rrrrrrrrrrring.

"Just a minute," I called out.

As I looked through the peephole in the door I bit down hard on the tip of my tongue. What a wonderful invention, the peephole. It has saved me from many awkward situations in the past. Peering through blearily, I saw to my horror that it was Mrs. Crabtree. I slowly opened the door and prepared for the onslaught I knew was coming. I bit my tongue again for good measure.

"Good morning Mrs. Crabtree. How may I help you?"

I noticed that she was in her usual nasty mood, her hair curlers wound tight to her scalp, and ready for battle.

"I have an emergency," she announced.

"I'm sorry to hear that, what is the problem?"

"I have a leak," she spat.

"What is leaking Mrs. Crabtree?"

"My faucet is leaking," she hissed.

157

"I will come up and have a look as soon as I am dressed," I offered.

"I'll wait," she said, glaring at me.

Instead of saying what was struggling to escape my lips, I bit my tongue once more, closed the door, pulled on a pair of pants, struggled into a shirt, stepped into my loafers and prepared to accompany the crab up to her lair on the fourth floor. As we stepped into the elevator she bumped into another resident as she was getting out.

"Excuse me," said Mrs. Dracool, as the Crab sidled past her.

"Fat bitch," muttered the crab under her breath, as she stabbed the button for the fourth floor. As we entered her apartment the strong aroma of cat urine immediately assaulted me with stomach churning ferocity. Fighting the intense urge to throw up the breakfast I had not eaten yet and the almost reflex, "Jesus, Mrs. Crabtree your pussy stinks!"

Instead I managed to say, with eyes streaming,

"Which faucet?"

"The kitchen," she snarled.

I went toward the kitchen, carefully stepping over the cat's bowl and stood in front of the sink.

Tightening the handle, the drip slowed considerably, almost to a stop.

"The drip is much slower now" I began, but was interrupted

with a shrill, "See! It's still dripping."

"Call your plumber in the morning and he will change the washers for you." I advised.

"This is an emergency, I want it done now!" she shrieked, the veins in her neck bulging dangerously.

"A dripping faucet is not an emergency Mrs. Crabtree," I explained and left the scene of the crime.

Back in the sanctuary of my apartment my first stop was the shower. I stayed in an extra ten minutes hoping that the stink of the cat urine would be fully washed off. With a fresh cup of coffee in hand I sat on the steps outside my kitchen door and took in the heady scent of the lavender bushes that grew in profusion around the edge of the pathway. I was very fortunate to live on the ground floor and had the added bonus of a side entrance. As I sat there sipping the aromatic coffee and thinking how lucky I was, a momentary flash of white accompanied by rustling noises in the shrubbery grabbed my attention. At first I couldn't see anything but, as I peered, *there it was again*, a white flash and a scurry of movement. I was about to get up to investigate when my phone rang and I went inside to answer it. I checked the caller I.D. and saw that it was one of the many tele-marketers who regularly call me trying to sell something. I ignored the ringing and instead decided to finally to do my long overdue laundry.

Laundry, as any man will attest, is a nightmare task that unfortunately must be undertaken. No use in trying to ignore it as the pile only gets higher. I confess that I have, on occasion, dumped the whole pile of underwear, socks, and tees and bought everything anew rather than hunt for coins and schlep the odorous bag to the basement. Armed with a pile of coins and the bag slung over my shoulder I now had a choice to make. The laundry room was in the basement so I could either take the elevator or walk down the stairs. Simple choice you might think. But as the early morning entanglement with Mrs. Crabtree was still fresh in my mind, I feared getting in the elevator lest I meet her again and have no immediate means of escape, I felt that the stairs were my best option. At least then I could hear anyone else on the stairs and a quick peek over the handrail would alert me to the identity of the approaching individual and, if necessary, I could perform an evasive maneuver. The trip to the laundry room passed uneventfully and with a furtive glance I saw the room was empty. I hurriedly loaded the machine and withdrew silently. I crept upstairs noiselessly and entered my apartment. This game of cat and mouse would resume every thirty minutes when I would have to put the wet clothes in the dryer, and then once more to retrieve them.

Back safely in my apartment I brewed another cup of coffee and turned on the CD player, hit the shuffle button, and let the music gods decide. Soon the familiar strains of the piano intro to *Riders on the Storm*, that classic song by the Doors, filled the room. As I sat there immersed in the music and lulled by Jim Morrison's hypnotic voice I remembered the open kitchen door. I got up, went to the kitchen, and closed it. As I turned around and walked back toward the living room, a scurry of movement under the couch caught my eye.
"That's odd," I thought as I got on my knees to look underneath. It was dark under there but I could see enough to know that it was a small wild rabbit.

As I sat there on the floor looking at the long eared visitor I realized that it had made a determined effort to get in my apartment. Outside the kitchen door there are six steps leading down to the small garden area. This meant that the baby bunny had to climb those steps, hop over the threshold, scamper the length of the kitchen, enter the hallway, make a left turn, continue down the hallway, enter the living room, traverse across the floor, and finally, hide under my old, sagging couch. No mean feat for an adolescent lupine, unfamiliar with the territory! The next thought to cross my puzzled mind was, *why*? Was it a sign? If so, was it a good sign? I knew that carrying a rabbit's foot supposedly brings good luck to the bearer and now I had all four, plus the owner of the feet. *Maybe I should go out and play the lottery,* I mused. *Maybe it was sent to me to remind me of the rabbits I had chased relentlessly as a young boy, with my dog Lassie, all those long years ago. Maybe it was the reincarnation of a rabbit that I had scared out of its wits in a field in Ireland. Maybe it was Karma. and now I would have to feed and care for it for life, and in retribution for my cruelty to its forebears. What if it was a magic rabbit, just like in Alice in Wonderland, and was sent to bring me to meet the Mad Hatter?*

My reverie was interrupted when a twitching nose poked out from under the couch and looked up at me in wonderment. Lettuce, I thought, she wants lettuce! I searched the refrigerator to no avail. Nothing. No lettuce. No carrots, nothing green whatsoever. Looking around the kitchen I spotted a box of Ritz crackers on the table. *Well, it's worth a try,* I supposed. Sitting on the floor again I offered a single, garlic flavored Ritz cracker to the starving bunny and was surprised when it took it from my hand, nibbled on it, and was soon looking for another. It was literally eating out of my hand and by the time the third cracker was devoured, I was allowed to pick her up. That was the start of the love affair with Sasha.

Sasha? I hear you ask. Well, it's all to do with the big brown eyes you see. She reminded me of a beautiful Russian girl I once knew and hence the name, but that's another story for another time. Suffice to say, Sasha and I have lived happily together now for four years, and no, I did not win the lottery, and yes, she does eat me out of house and home, but I forgive her for that every time I see her gaze at me with those big, dreamy, brown eyes. Later that afternoon I remembered my laundry and went to retrieve it. To my surprise, I found it on the table neatly sorted and folded. Maybe Sasha had something to do with it?

John A. Brennan

Chasing the Jaguar

The Inca civilization rose from the highlands of Peru sometime in the early 13th century, and the last Inca stronghold was conquered by the Spanish in 1572. From 1438 to 1533, the Inca used a variety of methods, from conquest to peaceful assimilation, to incorporate a large portion of western South America, centered on the Andean mountain ranges, including, besides Peru, large parts of modern Ecuador, western and south central Bolivia, northwest Argentina, north, and central Chile, and a small part of southern Columbia.[11] To the Inca, the Jaguar represented royalty and power.

I arrived in Guayaquil, a fishing port on the east coast of Ecuador, on a hot, steamy afternoon in mid-July. The descending twin prop flew in ever decreasing circles to avoid the jagged Andean peaks as it approached the airport. The purpose of my visit was to explore Quito, the old capital city of the country, which has the unique distinction of straddling the equator and is the oldest Spanish colonial city in South America. Then, when the tourist in me was sated I would make the journey to Cuenca, a market town nestled high up in the mountains. After a brief stop at Otavalo, the small town noted for its leather goods and silver ornaments I would continue my adventure by canoe, down the Agua Rico River to where it flows into Lake Imuya.

After crossing the lake I planned to enter the jungle in search of the elusive jaguar. The river forms a borderline between Ecuador and its neighbor Peru. Regular skirmishes flare up between the two countries, and full scale war has erupted more than once. The plan was to set off early

---

[11] "Inca Empire." *Wikipedia: The Free Encyclopedia*. Wikimedia Foundation Inc., 06 Mar. 2014. Web. 12 Mar. 2013

from the Indian village, located a mile or so from the grassy banks of the river, so named for the gold deposits found there, and which the Inca used to make their exquisite adornments. The Spanish invaders, led by the conquistador Francisco Pizzaro, named it the *rich river* soon after they discovered it on one of their many deadly forays against the Inca. They were in search of *El Dorado* the much rumored, mythical city of gold.

I first met Pascal, a descendant of the Inca, in the hotel bar in Cuenca and told him of my desire to see the jaguar. He listened intently and then asked,
"Which one?"
"What do you mean which one?" I enquired, puzzled.
"There are two species. The normal spotted jaguar and the much rarer black one."

My excitement grew on hearing this and I told him that I would be happy seeing either one. He motioned to two of his Indian friends who were sitting at the far end of the bar and they joined us at our table. A deal was struck whereby for a fee they would be my guides. We all shook hands and drank several toasts to the jaguar. By the end of the night the tequila bottles were empty save for the worms, and the Indians had jokingly christened me *Senor Fawcett*. Percy Fawcett, the famous British explorer, had mysteriously disappeared in 1925 on one of his many expeditions through the Brazilian rainforest. He was in search of the lost city of Z. I laughed nervously at this and hoped that I would fare better than poor old Fawcett.

Most of that night is dreamlike, but I recall brief flashes of coherence, and singing Irish rebel songs at the top of my lungs, with the Indians dancing and falling about the floor, and a lot of laughter. They told me later

163

that I had climbed up on the table to make a speech, and insisted that they were to accompany me to Ireland to help me fight the British. They promised that they would, and bring their bows and arrows. I, in turn swore that I would help them fight their enemies, the Peruvians, and boasted that I would and could do it single handedly. After that, all else is blurred and lost in the alcoholic haze.

I rose to the surface slowly the next morning lying face down in a hammock. I was somewhere in the middle of the jungle, with the merciless screeching of parrots ringing in my tortured skull. My face was inches from the ground and I could see a swarm of huge soldier ants trooping off toward the opposite wall. With visions of being eaten alive, in panic, I struggled to turn over and re-position my aching corpse right side up. It was then that I silently cursed tequila in particular and all alcoholic beverages in general and swore fervently, should I survive this descent into hell, never to drink again. As my eyes began their slow agonizing return to focus, I realized that I was in a small mud hut with a dirt floor, and a thatched roof.

Soon, Pascal entered through the small doorway holding a wooden bowl. He was wearing a headdress of brightly colored feathers and a grass skirt. I had the sudden thought that I might have insulted one of his daughters the previous night and now he was going to poison me. But no, he was smiling and offering me the bowl. I waved him away with a feeble, "No thanks. I think I'm dying," and covered my eyes wishing I was somewhere else. He was persistent, so I slowly sat up and took a few sips. In no time the bowl was empty and within minutes I was miraculously rejuvenated.

"What was that? You must give me the recipe."

"I can't Irishman, it's a tribal secret, and if I tell you I will have to cook and eat you," he joked.

We left the village at daybreak and walked along the old, time worn trail to the edge of the river where the dugouts were moored. After selecting the biggest and most sturdy one we placed our backpacks inside along with cases of water, a basket of assorted fruits and dried meat, then pushed it into the water and set off. We rowed for the rest of that day, pausing briefly at times to rest, eat, and drink water. Occasionally, Cayman could be seen basking on the banks, their prehistoric, reptilian eyes watching us intently as we floated past.

At one point in the journey we passed large military encampments on each side of the river and I could see both countries flags waving proudly in the gentle breeze. Pascal explained that these were border lookout posts and as the area was rich with gold deposits, unlawful digging was deterred by the military presence. Laughing, he pointed to the Peruvian soldiers manning their post, and reminded me of my boasting the night before. I tactfully ignored the taunts, and pretended to search my backpack for something very important.

"Maybe on the way back," I lied.

I got the feeling that they didn't believe me.

After several hours of rowing, we came to a particular place on the river where the water suddenly changes its color from the natural greenish blue to almost black. This dramatic change manifests as a perfect line across the surface, as if drawn by an invisible hand. I was puzzled by this sudden change in color and was told it was due to the high *tannin* content in the trees that washed into the river along small tributaries. Large downed branches and huge amounts of jungle brush are also washed into the river during tropical storms, and could make our journey more hazardous. We rowed for many more hours, then decided that as nightfall was near and not wanting to be on the river after dark we would make camp on the bank and continue toward the lake in the morning. Before daybreak we set off once more, but soon found our way blocked by a mass of floating branches and vegetation. We spent at least an hour cutting our way through and finally, after another hour of rowing we floated out onto the surface of the largest, and most beautiful, calm lake I had ever seen.

The long drawn out *whoop* of a howler monkey shattered the silence, and echoed all around us. As the echo faded the silence dropped again, slowly. The stillness enveloping the lake that morning was perfect. The air, pure and cold, could be tasted. Traces of the wispy, low lying mist that hung just above the surface were slowly evaporating as the sun climbed lazily in the eastern sky. The flatness of the lake was a mirrored expanse stretching away from our canoe in all directions, and the reflection of a small, tree covered Island floating aimlessly off in the distance was crystal clear on the cold, azure water. A shimmering, pink skinned, freshwater dolphin broke smoothly from the depths and seemed to smile at us as it arched and slid gently back under.

I glanced over my shoulder and smiled at the Indians sitting behind as they rowed with easy, practiced strokes, and watched as the ripples ran off from the sides of the dugout and disappear in the distance, as if in a hurry to reach the shore. The lush, green, canopied jungle lay up ahead and I wondered if I would finally get to see the rare, fabled Jaguar once venerated by the Inca. Pascal had assured me that I would, but I knew it would not be easy as the big cats lived deep in the interior, and we would have to re-cut an old trail. Trails are quickly overgrown due to the high humidity, copious rainfall, and tropical heat, which is the perfect recipe for fast growth. Some species of vine can grow as much as six feet in one day. My sharpened machete lay in the bottom of the canoe at my feet.

Up front, Pascal raised his hand as a signal for us to stop rowing. I raised my oar, and as the canoe glided slowly to a halt, he handed me the binoculars and pointed. I raised the glasses and focused on a spot off in the direction of his outstretched arm. A large flock of birds were coming our way, too far off to see clearly, but as I adjusted the glasses and they got nearer, I saw that they were Macaws. The sky became a riot of scarlet colored flashes as their wings beat through the air. As they passed noisily overhead and flew off in the direction of the island, I continued to follow them, and watched as they lit in the treetops. The Indians prized the bright red feathers of the Macaw and used them for their colorful headdresses. We resumed rowing then, and the lake was silent once more broken only by the gentle splash of our oars as they dipped in and out of the water.

We stepped out of the dugout at a less dense area of shoreline, pulled it up on high ground, and tied it securely to the base of a sturdy tree. As we walked into the jungle the heat, at first, was oppressive, the coolness of the lake by then, a distant memory. Pascal cut the vines and hanging branches and as we followed we cut the ones he missed. We were now well inside the rainforest and the humidity was almost overpowering.
We had brought plenty of water and Pascal had told me that he knew of a freshwater stream should we get low. The sunlight faded dramatically as we progressed further in, and it took a while for our eyes to become accustomed to the interior darkness. The area was made up of mahogany trees, their large, smooth trunks stretching majestically skyward, and I wondered if any of the wood I had worked with in my other life as a carpenter, had come from this region.

A sudden loud scampering sound and branches being shaken made us all look up. There, high up in the canopy, was a troop of noisy spider monkeys on their way to another feeding area, probably a fig tree. They took no notice of us as they swung from tree to tree, intent on their evening meal. Large colorful butterflies were our constant companions as they fluttered all around, in search of nectar. Soon, we came to a small clearing where shafts of fading sunlight lit the ground and turned the whole area into a serene, breathtaking oasis. Sure enough, as Pascal had said, a gurgling stream wound its way through the clearing, cascaded over the rocks, and flowed off into the jungle again, on its way to the lake, its final destination.

We decided to make camp there and a good dry spot was chosen. We hung our hammocks between the trees, close together and then prepared a fire pit. As we sat around the fire eating a strong stew containing I knew not what, nor dared ask, we chatted and joked like old friends. I found out later that the main ingredient in the stew was a mixture of cayman and guinea pig meat. Finally we all clambered into our hammocks and settled down for the night, the fire heaped with enough fuel to last until morning. As I lay there in the soft folds of the hammock lulled by the gentle swaying, a lone cicada started making her night calls. Soon a second joined in and then a third. Before long the jungle was alive with the evening chorus and as I listened it became clear that they were following a distinct, pre-ordained pattern. The sound rose and fell rhythmically and seemed to ebb and flow through the warm night air. After about an hour it rose to a deafening crescendo, and then abruptly stopped. The silence was complete once more.
Sometime during the night I thought I heard a low, growling sound off in the deep reaches, but I wasn't sure. I had fallen into a deep slumber, and dreamt of the Jaguar.

What time it was when I awoke, I don't know but it was before dawn and still dark. Every muscle in my body was aching from rowing and slashing at the undergrowth over the previous couple of days. I glanced at my companions as they slept and listened to their light snores, and I could hear the faint, comforting, splashing sound of the stream as it caressed the rocks, on its way past the camp. The fire had burned low but still gave off light and heat and as I lay there waiting for my eyes to become adjusted, I was suddenly alerted by a rustling sound off to my left. I sat up, turned my head slowly, rubbed my eyes, and stared. I could make out a slight movement at the tree line, close to where the stream entered the jungle. As I focused I saw two large, bright yellow eyes staring at me. *It can't be!* With as little movement as possible, I instinctively reached for my knapsack, slid my hand into the front pocket, and closed my fingers around the grip of the old Webley pistol that I had placed there prior to leaving the village. As I slowly brought it up level, from behind a hand grabbed my wrist and another covered my mouth.

"*Shhh! be very still Irishman.*" It was Pascal. How he had managed to creep up without me hearing him I'll never know, he had that uncanny knack of appearing and disappearing at will. "You wanted to see the jaguar Irishman, well, now you will. He has come to visit with you," he whispered. As we both watched, the huge cat crept closer, looked at us fearlessly, and padded silently toward the stream. He was no more than twenty feet from where we sat, transfixed. I could now see him clearly, and I watched spellbound as his glossy, black coat undulated with each silent step. My heart pounded as I saw the muscles across his shoulders ripple with each measured movement that spoke to the hidden power within his large frame. He crossed the stream, and only then did he feel safe enough to drink. He was facing us directly, and spreading his front paws bent down and lapped at the water. As he lapped, I could see his four inch long fangs gleaming in the light from the fading fire. Occasionally he raised his head and gazed in our direction holding us with his large, tawny eyes.

I was riveted but strangely unafraid, and felt privileged to be in the presence of this symbol of royalty, and master of the jungle. He turned abruptly then and silently padded off into the early morning, and was gone. I was so thrilled by the whole experience and as I lay awake in the hammock thought of my father

Well Mal, that's another potential regret waylaid.

Ecuador - Lake Imuya and the Floating Island (1994)

John in Ecuador (1994)

The Prediction

The galactic line up, predicted by the Mayan astrologers, occurred
on December 21, 2012, the winter solstice. It does not predict the end
of the world; it foretells a new beginning. Extremes of weather and violent
seismic activity will occur at the onset of this new period. Globally, there
will be much political unrest and violence. This is a warning for us that
we must change our ways. This line up happens once every 26,500
years and could be observed from Juan Fernandez Island
in the Pacific Ocean.[12]

Ninety one steps on each side set,
and the number of sides is four.
Add the platform on the high crest,
then three sixty five is the score.

It has always been done in this very way,
the last count to keep evermore.
To separate the night from the day,
the ancients who knew it for sure.

The ball court where life was mere play,
is silent and now used no more.
Where the ghost still holds its sway,
with bright, keen eyes, trained on the shore.

Their calendar holds bare truth sere,
in bactun, long count, and much more.

---

[12] "2012 Phenomenon." *Wikipedia: The Free Encyclopedia*. Wikimedia Foundation
Inc., 24 Mar. 2014. Web. 10 Mar. 2013

John A. Brennan

Of the future from this very year,
the way is now clear, they are sure.

The orbs in the heavens are near,
they now dance to the rhythm of time.
And so it becomes crystal clear,
when the Sun and the dark rift align.

If we don't find the path and reform,
the Ancients will not heed our plea.
We must learn to live as when born,
or on our heads a sad plight they'll decree.

The oceans will wash o'er the land,
and the heavens will darken and cry.
The earth it will shake to bare sands,
and the mountains will crumble and die.

Back When

Back when Brian Jones, the maestro, the golden haired illusionist

drowned in his lone supplication. The little red rooster crowing aloud.

The Rolling Stone who refused to gather moss. Time not on his side.

Back when John Lennon imagined that all we needed was love,

but taking the bullet instead near the strawberry field.

"Mother, you had me, but I never had you," he cried.

Back when Janis Joplin, the perfect, shining pearl, was dulled by

her own private crucifixion. At full tilt in a Mercedes Benz,

foot to the floor. Her heart shattered in a thousand pieces.

Back when Keith Moon died before he got old.

Out in one last triumphant drumroll.

Back when George Harrison rode the quiet, dark horse and went

to play for his sweet Lord, his guitar gently weeping.

Back when Kurt Cobain, saddened but no more in sufferance,

took the last red eye to his own private Nirvana, his refuge.

Back when Amy, the black butterfly fluttered and faded, and went

back to black.

Pyramid of the Moon Teotihuacan, Mexico (1996)

CHAPTER 8

On Reflection

The Age Spot

A sharp intake of breath was my first reaction as I looked in the bathroom mirror one morning. I stopped mid shave, blinked and stared, incredulous. There must be some mistake. I dried my hands and put on my glasses, which only showed it more clearly. I quickly removed them and set them on the sink. Maybe if I scratched it would go away.

But no, it still remained and would be with me forever, from this day forward. I rubbed my eyes frantically and stared again. Yes, there it sat, very comfortable looking, like an unwanted guest who had decided to move in permanently. An age spot!

A long moment of panic gripped me like an ice cold vise as it slowly dawned on me that there was a faint possibility that I, me, myself might be getting old. Jesus! I thought, next thing, I'll be looking for Viagra and a penis pump!

'But I'm much too young to get old,' I reasoned, in silent desperation. 'Maybe it's just a freckle.'

It was just the other day when I got off the train at Marble Arch and with winged feet, quickly covered the short distance past Speaker's corner, arriving at Hyde Park. In reality it was the summer of 1969. I was eighteen and had arrived in London in June that year, from Ireland. Shoulder length hair, bell bottom jeans, a tie-dyed T-shirt, leather jacket and several strands of beads around my neck. I was ready for action!

As I strode along brimming with that heady arrogance of youth and neared the park, I could hear the music loud and clear. The sweet, pungent aroma of marijuana, mingling with the sensual scent of sandalwood incense, wafted invitingly on the cool, London air. Soon I was there among the faithful, five hundred thousand strong.

The familiar green lawn in the center of the park was gone, replaced by a multitude of moving and swaying bodies from all over Europe and beyond, intent on creating and absorbing good feelings. An ocean of colorful banners fluttered in the gentle breeze that blew in from the Thames, caressed the trees, crossed the Serpentine, and brushed our smiling faces. Many had guitars and tambourines and were making their own music as they waited. Peace signs were everywhere, on flags, on arm bands and even painted on faces. Peace and love was all that mattered to us and the music tied it all together.

Even though the circumstances surrounding the event were based in sadness, we all saw it as a celebration of a great soul. Three days earlier, on July 3 the world froze in disbelief, as word spread that Brian Jones had died. Jones was the founding member of the Rolling Stones and had been fired one month earlier, a victim to his drug problem and irascible behavior. He was found in the bottom of his swimming pool at his home just outside London, the house formerly owned by A. A. Milne. He was just 27 years old and we were all stunned and saddened by the loss of so great a musician. Little did we know then that he would be one of many to join what became known as the *Twenty- Seven* club. Brian was equally revered for his musical mastery and his boyish good looks. It was easy to see why the girls went limp limbed at the mere mention of his name. The long blond hair cascading around his shoulders and the piercing grey/green eyes made him appear godlike to them.

As for music, he could play anything. Lead guitar, sitar, dulcimer, and everything else with strings. He had run off to Scandinavia at age sixteen to play guitar and when he returned to London he brought with him a completely new sound. That innovation in sound ensured that the Stones would lead the music scene for the next fifty years.

The concert had been set in motion two weeks before Brian died and was meant to introduce the new lead guitarist, Mick Taylor, the chosen replacement. We all had our doubts about that.

'Taylor is an ace with a guitar,' the press releases announced in advance. Maybe he was, but by the end of that memorable day, we would know. He had played with John Mayall's Bluesbreakers, for a few years so maybe he would be Ok.

I was brimming with excitement because I was going to see a girl I had met the previous day as I strolled down the center of the world, *Carnaby Street*. I was trying on a bright red military style jacket that was hanging on a rack outside one of the many *hip* stores. Jimi Hendrix wore one just like it and I was posing and posturing in front of a large mirror when I noticed a girl trying on a big pink floppy hat, outside the store next door. She was eyeing me up and down.

"I don't have horns, do I?" I asked, sarcastically.

"I don't think so," she answered, "unless they're invisible."

I laughed and said, "I like that hat," using my real cool voice.

"Are you going to buy it for me," she teased.

"I will if you show me your tits."

I bought the hat. I was a pushover then and still am. She told me her name was Michelle and said she was from Paris. We arranged to meet up in the park the day of the concert. She loved the Rolling Stones too and promised me that as soon as Mick Jagger came on the stage, she would remove her top. Talk about the luck of the Irish! I couldn't wait!

I told her I would see her in the park next to the *upside down* tree at noon, and as we parted she said, "Adieu, Irishman," with her velvety French accent and gave me the look that girls give you. You know the *look* I mean.

The next day, as I wound my way down through the sea of gyrating humanity I could hear the familiar voice of Robert Fripp, lead singer of the band *King Crimson* as they finished their set with the classic, *Court of the Crimson King*. Sure enough, there was Michelle under the tree, sitting cross legged on the grass eating an apple, waiting for me. "Alo," she called waving and as I dropped down beside her on the lawn I stole a furtive glance at her sweater. "Do you want a bite?" she asked, offering me the apple. I looked at her and smiled saying, "I don't think I should, I might get in trouble." We both laughed and after chatting for a while, the apple eaten, we made our way toward the stage and jostled through until we found a good spot about 100 feet from the front. The stagehands were setting up the equipment for the Stones who were due to appear at around one o'clock. We all were ready to rock and the anticipation could be tasted. Joints were passed around with great regularity, and I remember thinking how great it would be if this feeling could somehow be made to last forever. There was a great sense of togetherness that day.

We believed that the music would truly set us free, and in some way, shield us from that other world of madness, violence, and pain. Even though it was a sad occasion the mood in the park that afternoon was joyful. Even the distant carnage in Viet Nam would not dampen our spirits. Nearer to home, what would become a long, protracted, and extremely violent war was gaining momentum on the streets of Belfast and Derry, as the Irish civil rights movement took to the streets. But none of that mattered then, we were in a different place and were determined to show

180

the rest of the world that we could all get along together.

A fanfare of trumpets wafted out from the loudspeakers over our heads and we knew it was about to begin. All eyes turned toward the stage and there he was; a vision in a full length, white Kaftan, long hair hanging below his shoulders. He walked, unusually sedate for him, to the microphone and opened a book that he held in his hands. I was in awe and forgot all about the sweater and the promise. Mick Jagger was now the only thing that mattered. He was our link with Brian.

"Peace, peace. He is not dead, he doth sleep,"

he read, quoting from Adonais, the beautiful poem that Percy Shelley had written and dedicated to his great friend John Keats.

"He lives he wakes, 'tis death is dead, not he. Weep not for Adonais."

It was a moving tribute to Brian and at the end of the reading thousands of white butterflies were released to soar above our heads. As we craned our necks and followed their flight it was one of those perfect moments. We could imagine Brian's soul going aloft with them and being at peace. As I brought my head back around to face the stage, I gasped, there they were! Right there in front of me. I had almost missed them! Michelle had kept her promise and was proudly displaying her perfect, milky white, French breasts, resplendent in the afternoon sun. Much too soon, in a flash, her top was back on and I wondered if it had all been a dream. But no, it was real and as the distinctive Keith Richards sharp guitar licks rang out loud and clear and Bill Wymans bass thundered with freight train ferocity and Charlie Watts drums roared and Mick Taylor coaxed unheard of crystal clear notes from his *Gibson*, and Jagger strutted and wheeled like a dervish, a deafening roar of pure joy emanated from the crowd, and we all sang along to our anthem until we were hoarse, *I can't get no satisfaction.*

Michelle told me that just as the butterflies were being released, so were her breasts and that if I was a good boy she might show them to me again, later. I can assure you that I was an extremely good boy for the rest of that day. I thought that it was so fitting and so apt, and was so taken with the whole experience, I fell in love at that moment with everyone and everything including the girl from Paris. I was satisfied that day for sure and Mick Taylor was accepted by us all.

On the way out of the park later that evening, I climbed the *upside down* tree and declared my love aloud, for the girl from Paris, with no regrets.

The Prophet

I had the great pleasure of meeting Bob Marley in London in the early seventies.
I was in his presence for perhaps fifteen minutes. In that time he managed
to convey to me a deep philosophy that has remained with me until this day.
He said to me "Man, every conversation be a revelation."

From old nine mile in Saint Anne town,
his soul now flies at peace and free.
The Rasta man with his vision found,
a world of pure simplicity.

Redemption Song, let freedom ring,
Three Little Birds on the doorstep.
Now we don't worry about a thing,
this is the faith that I have kept.

In old Trenchtown one love blesses all,
Dunn's river fall, the sweetest pain.
No Woman No Cry, not be small,
the *Exodus*, it begin again.

In London town I met a man,
dreadlocked all long and swinging free.
He told me of his simple plan,
a world in perfect harmony

Every conversation that pass between
revelations we must surely glean.
No matter class nor shade of skin
we must unite and cleanse all sin.

Jah! Music man as all will see,
I sing my song from heartfelt core.
The reggae version is the key,
I lay it all at your front door.

From Kingston town to Buff bay blue,
and Jamaica Inn where I did lay,
I felt his soul caress my face
and whisper words from far away.

Haile Selassie in sweet Africa,
his ring he gave it onto me.
The Judah lion, the word of Jah,
a sign for all humanity.

The shanty town where I was born
rings loud with song of my degree.
And fills the world from night to morn,
my light and soul will set you free.

Every talk is the word of Jah,
who watches all and holds His sway.
From Irishtown to America,
sweet peace and love is the only way.

John A. Brennan

Back When

They're all dust in the wind now. Aloft, crying, beseeching, departed,
everlasting, but loved.
But through it all there was always St. Michael and always Jesus,
watching, protecting and suffering alongside. My guides. My mentors.
My forgiving saviors. With me as I crossed unfamiliar oceans,
wasted deserts and ancient valleys drowned in the dust of ages past,
ever seeking. Finding myself back at the familiar cross roads.
Puzzled, stupefied and bewildered, but safe.
And I'm still standing here, waiting. And you know what?
I still know nothing, but I have no regrets.

The author in Jamaica, B.W.I.

Epilogue

"Son."
"What dad?"
"Whatever you do, don't die with regrets."
"Don't worry dad, I won't."

John A. Brennan

About The Author

John Anthony Brennan is a native of Crossmaglen, a small town in County Armagh, Ireland. He left his beloved, sacred green isle many moons ago to see the world and has been island hopping ever since. He once lived on another island called Manhattan, which he calls *the largest open air lunatic asylum on the planet*. He finally escaped to the sanctuary of the Long Island just in time to save his sanity, or so he thought. He was trained as a master carpenter but soon after arriving in New York he changed career and studied to become a building manager. He managed a residential property on prestigious Park Avenue for many years.

The urge to travel and explore the cultures and sacred places of the ancient peoples has always been his driving force. Starting in 1993 he was fortunate enough to have the opportunity to do just that. He spent seven years traveling and absorbed the energies he believes emanates from all sacred sites. From Newgrange in the Boyne Valley in Ireland, Stonehenge in England, the Mayan and Aztec temples scattered throughout South America and the colossal pyramids in Egypt, he has visited them all and is convinced that a common thread connects them. He incorporates his experiences in his works and some of his writing expresses a spiritual dimension.

Made in the USA
Charleston, SC
23 August 2014